DISASTE
MANAGEMENT

Published by:
Saurabh Publishing House

DISASTER MANAGEMENT

Mukesh Kapoor

Publishing House
4735/22, Prakash Deep Building,
Ansari Road, Daryaganj,
New Delhi - 110002

Published by
SAURABH PUBLISHING HOUSE

Distributed by:
Lotus Press Publishers & Distributors
Unit No. 220, Second Floor, 4735/22, Prakash Deep Building,
Ansari Road, Darya Ganj, New Delhi-110002
Ph.: 011-23280047, 32903912, 9811838000
E-mail: lotus_press@sify.com, www.lotuspress.co.in

Saurabh Publishing House is an imprint of
Lotus Press Publishers & Distributors

ISBN: 978-81-89005-62-7

Printed at: Concept Imprint, Delhi

Preface

Disaster management refers to the discipline which is involved in the mitigation and management of risks involved in both the pre- and post-disaster scenarios. As both human-made as well as natural disasters in the world occur with greater frequency in the world, the import that the discipline carries cannot be stressed enough. Effective emergency management relies on thorough integration of emergency plans at all levels of government and non-government involvement. Activities at each level (individual, group, community) affect the other levels; disaster management thereby is a crucial step in understanding and putting into action all that is needed to bring a disastrous situation under control.

The present text is an effort in the step to bring under the reader's attention all that is needed to know about disaster management. The effort behind the design of the book is to not just enable readers to formulate the ideas behind disaster management, i. e., mitigation, preparedness, response and recovery, but also foster an understanding of how the field works within the framework of both national and international agencies. A special area of focus is the case-studies which seek to give a pragmatic understanding of disaster management, along with an assessment of the challenges and risks it presents. It is hoped that the incisive and comprehensive content of the book serves well for all Any suggestions for further improvement are most welcome.

Author

CONTENTS

1

Disaster: An Introduction

Disaster is the tragedy of a natural or human-made hazard that negatively affects society or environment. In contemporary academia, disasters are seen as the consequence of inappropriately managed risk. These risks are the product of hazards and vulnerability. Hazards that strike in areas with low vulnerability are not considered a disaster, as is the case in uninhabited regions.

Developing countries suffer the greatest costs when a disaster hits – more than 95 percent of all deaths caused by disasters occur in developing countries, and losses due to natural disasters are 20 times greater (as a percentage of GDP) in developing countries than in industrialised countries.

A disaster can be defined as any tragic event that may involve at least one victim of circumstance, such as an accident, fire, terrorist attack, or explosion. Disaster is a sudden, calamitous event bringing great damage, loss, and destruction and devastation to life and property. The damage caused by disasters is immeasurable and varies with the geographical location, climate and the type of the earth surface/degree of vulnerability. This influences the mental, socio-economic, political and cultural state of the affected area. Generally, disaster has the following effects in the concerned areas.

1. It completely disrupts the normal day to day life.
2. It negatively influences the emergency systems.
3. Normal needs and processes like food, shelter, health, etc. are affected and deteriorate depending on the intensity and severity of the disaster.

It may also be termed as "a serious disruption of the functioning of society, causing widespread human, material or environmental losses which exceed the ability of the affected society to cope using its own resources."

Thus, a disaster may have the following main features:

- Unpredictability
- Unfamiliarity
- Speed
- Urgency
- Uncertainty
- Threat

TYPES OF DISASTERS

Generally, disasters are of two types – Natural and Man-made. Based on the devastation, these are further classified into major/minor natural disasters and major/minor man-made disasters. Some of the disasters are listed below:

- Major natural disasters:
  - Flood
  - Cyclone
  - Drought
  - Earthquake

- Minor natural disasters:
  - Cold wave
  - Thunderstorms
  - Heat waves
  - Mud slides
  - Storm
- Major man-made disasters:
  - Setting of fires
  - Epidemic
  - Deforestation
  - Pollution due to prawn cultivation
  - Chemical pollution
  - Wars
- Minor man-made disasters:
  - Road/train accidents, riots
  - Food poisoning
  - Industrial disaster/crisis
  - Environmental pollution

Risk is a measure of the expected losses due to a hazardous event of a particular magnitude occurring in a given area over a specific time period. Risk is a function of the probability of particular occurrences and the losses each would cause. The level of risk depends on:

- Nature of the Hazard
- Vulnerability of the elements which are affected
- Economic value of those elements

It is defined as "the extent to which a community, structure, service, and/or geographic area is likely to be damaged or disrupted by the impact of particular hazard, on account of their nature, construction and proximity to hazardous terrain or a disaster prone area."

The extent of damage in a disaster depends on:

(1) The impact, intensity and characteristics of the phenomenon, and

(2) How people, environment and infrastructures are affected by that phenomenon.

This relationship can be written as an equation:

Disaster Risk = Hazard + Vulnerability

For more than a century researchers have been studying disasters and for more than fifty years disaster research has been institutionalised through the Disaster Research Center in U.S. The studies reflect a common opinion when they argue that all disasters can be seen as being human-made, their reasoning being that human actions before the strike of the hazard can prevent it developing into a disaster. All disasters are hence the result of human failure to introduce appropriate disaster management measures. Hazards are routinely divided into natural or human-made, although complex disasters, where there is no single root cause, are more common in developing countries. A specific disaster may spawn a secondary disaster that increases the impact. A classic example is an earthquake that causes a tsunami, resulting in coastal flooding.

Natural Disasters

Natural disaster is the consequence of a natural hazard (e.g. volcanic eruption, earthquake, or landslide) which affects human activities. Human vulnerability, exacerbated by the lack of planning or appropriate emergency management, leads to financial, environmental or human losses. The resulting loss depends on the capacity of the population to support or resist the disaster, their resilience. This understanding is concentrated in the formulation: "disasters occur when hazards meet vulnerability". A natural hazard will hence never result in a natural disaster in areas without vulnerability, *e.g.* strong earthquakes in uninhabited areas. The term natural has consequently been disputed because the events simply are not hazards or disasters without human involvement.

Earthquake

Earthquake is an unexpected and rapid shaking of earth due to the breakage and shifting of underneath layers of Earth. Earthquake strikes all of a sudden at any time of day or night and quite violently. It gives no prior warning. If it happens in a populated area, the earthquake can cause great loss to human life and property.

Tornado

Tornado is one of the most violent storms on earth. It seems like a rotating and funnel shape cloud. It expands from the thunderstorm to the ground in the form of whirl winds reaching around 300 miles per hour. The damage path could move on to one mile wide and around 50 miles long. These storms can strike quickly without any warning.

Flood

Flood is also one of the most common hazards in India and some other parts of the world. The effects of a flood can be local to a neighbourhood or community. It can cast a larger impact, the whole river basin and multiple states could get affected. Every state is at its risk due to this hazard.

Water Damage

Water damage has a huge effect on your home, its neighbourhood and your city. It is very much necessary that you should prepare for water damage. You must know what should be done during and after water damage.

Hail

Hail comes into existence when updrafts in the thunder clouds take the raindrops up towards the extremely cold regions in the atmosphere. They freeze and combine forming lumps of ice. As these lumps can be very heavy and are not supported by the updraft, they fall off with the speeds of about 100 km per hour or more. A Hail is created in the form of an enormous cloud, commonly known as thunderheads.

Wildfire

Wild forest areas catching fire is a very big problem for the people who live around these areas. The dry conditions caused several times in the year in different parts of United States can increase the possibility for wildfires. If you are well prepared in advance and know how to protect the buildings in your area, you can reduce much of the damage caused by wildfire. It is everyone's duty to protect their home and neighbourhood from wildfire.

Hurricane

Hurricane also like the tornado is a wind storm, but it is a tropical cyclone. This is caused by a low pressure system that usually builds in the tropical. Huricanes comes with thunderstorms and a counterclockwise spread of winds near the surface of the earth.

Winter Freeze

Winter freeze storms are serious threats for people and their property. They include, snow, frozen rain, strong winds and extreme cold. Many precautions have to be taken in order to protect yourself, your family, home or property.

Lightning

Lightning is a much underestimated killer. Lightning is an abrupt electric expulsion which comes from cloud to cloud or from cloud to earth followed by an emission of light. Lightning is a common phenomenon after heavy rain and can also occur around 10 miles off from rainfall. Most lightning victims are people who are captivated outdoors in summer during the afternoon and evening.

Volcano

Volcano is a mountain that has an opening downwards to the reservoir of molten rock towards the surface of earth. Volcanoes are caused by the accrual of igneous products. As the pressure caused by gases in the molted rock becomes intense, the eruption takes place. The volcanic eruption can be of two kinds, quiet or volatile. The aftermaths of a volcano include flowing lava, flat landscapes, poisonous gases and fleeing ashes and rocks. Read on to know more on types of disasters.

Man-Made Disasters

Man-made disasters are events which, either intentionally or by accident cause severe threats to public health and well-being. Because their occurrence is unpredictable, man-made disasters pose an especially challenging threat that must be dealt with through vigilance, and proper preparedness and response. Information on the major sources of man-made disasters is provided here to help educate the public on their cause and effects as they relate to emergency planning.

Bioterrorism Attack

A bioterrorism attack is the deliberate release of viruses, bacteria, or other germs (agents) used to cause illness or death in people, animals, or plants. These agents are typically found in nature, but it is possible that they could be changed to increase their ability to cause disease, make them resistant to current medicines, or to increase their ability to be spread into the environment. Biological agents can be spread through the air, through water, or in food. Terrorists may use biological agents because they can be extremely difficult to detect and do not cause illness for several hours to several days. Some bioterrorism agents, like the smallpox virus, can be spread from person to person and some, like anthrax, can not.

Bioterrorism agents can be separated into three categories, depending on how easily they can be spread and the severity of illness or death they cause. Category A agents are considered the highest risk category B and Category C agents are those that are considered emerging threats for disease.

Category A

These high-priority agents include organisms or toxins that pose the highest risk to the public and national security because:

- They can be easily spread or transmitted from person to person.
- They result in high death rates and have the potential for major public health impact.
- They might cause public panic and social disruption.

— They require special action for public health preparedness.

Category B

These agents are the second highest priority because:

— They are moderately easy to spread.

— They result in moderate illness rates and low death rates.

— They require specific enhancements of CDC's laboratory capacity and enhanced disease monitoring.

Category C

These third highest priority agents include emerging pathogens that could be engineered for mass spread in the future because:

— They are easily available.

— They are easily produced and spread.

— They have potential for high morbidity and mortality rates and major health impact.

Chemical Emergency and Hazardous Chemicals

A chemical emergency occurs when a hazardous chemical has been released and the release has the potential for harming people's health. Chemical releases can be unintentional, as in the case of an industrial accident, or intentional, as in the case of a terrorist attack.

A chemical emergency occurs when a hazardous chemical has been released and the release has the potential for harming people's health. Chemical releases can be unintentional, as in the case of an industrial accident, or intentional, as in the case of a terrorist attack. Some chemicals that are hazardous have been developed by military organisations for use in warfare. Examples are nerve agents such as sarin and VX, mustards such as sulfur mustards and nitrogen mustards, and choking agents such as phosgene. It might be possible for terrorists to get these chemical warfare agents and use them to harm people.

Many hazardous chemicals are used in industry (for example, chlorine, ammonia, and benzene). Others are found in nature (for example, poisonous plants). Some could be made from everyday items such as household cleaners. These types of hazardous chemicals also could be obtained and used to harm people, or they could be accidentally released. Scientists often categorise hazardous chemicals by the type of chemical or by the effects a chemical would have on people exposed to it. In America, the categories/types used by the Centers for Disease Control and Prevention are as follows:

— *Biotoxins:* Poisons that come from plants or animals.

— *Blister agents/vesicants:* Chemicals that severely blister the eyes, respiratory tract, and skin on contact.

— *Blood agents*: Poisons that affect the body by being absorbed into the blood.

— *Caustics (acids)*: Chemicals that burn or corrode people's skin, eyes, and mucus membranes (lining of the nose, mouth, throat, and lungs) on contact.

— *Choking/lung/pulmonary agents*: Chemicals that cause severe irritation or swelling of the respiratory tract (lining of the nose and throat, lungs).

— *Incapacitating agents*: Drugs that make people unable to think clearly or that cause an altered state of consciousness (possibly unconsciousness).

— *Long-acting anticoagulants*: Poisons that prevent blood from clotting properly, which can lead to uncontrolled bleeding.

— *Metals*: Agents that consist of metallic poisons.

— *Nerve agents*: Highly poisonous chemicals that work by preventing the nervous system from working properly.

— *Organic solvents*: Agents that damage the tissues of living things by dissolving fats and oils.

— *Riot control agents/tear gas*: Highly irritating agents normally used by law enforcement for crowd control or by individuals for protection (for example, mace).

— *Toxic alcohols*: Poisonous alcohols that can damage the heart, kidneys, and nervous system.

— *Vomiting agents*: Chemicals that cause nausea and vomiting.

Pandemics and Diseases

A pandemic is a global disease outbreak. An influenza pandemic occurs when a new influenza virus emerges for which there is little or no immunity in the human population and the virus begins to cause serious illness and then spreads easily person-to-person worldwide.

A pandemic is a global disease outbreak. An influenza pandemic occurs when a new influenza A virus emerges for which there is little or no immunity in the human population and the virus begins to cause serious illness and then spreads easily person-to-person worldwide. The federal government, states, communities and industry are taking steps to prepare for and respond to an influenza pandemic.

If a pandemic occurs, it is likely to be a prolonged and widespread outbreak that could require temporary changes in many areas of society, such as schools, work, transportation and other public services. An informed and prepared public can take appropriate actions to decrease their risk during a pandemic. To be prepared for such an emergency, the authorities encourages individuals, businesses and communities to:

— Talk with your local public health officials and health care providers, who can supply information about the signs and symptoms of a specific disease outbreak and recommend prevention and control actions.

— Adopt business/school practices that encourage sick employees/students to stay home and anticipate how to function with a significant portion of the workforce/school population absent due to illness or caring for ill family members.

— Practice good health habits, including eating a balanced diet, exercising daily, and getting sufficient rest. In addition, take common-sense steps to stop the spread of germs including frequent hand washing, covering coughs and sneezes and staying away from others as much as possible when you are sick.

Radiation Emergencies and Event Management

Radiation is a form of energy that is present all around us. Different types of radiation exist, some of which have more energy than others. Amounts of radiation released into the environment are measured in units called curies. Radioactive materials are among the many kinds of hazardous substances emergency responders might have to deal with in a transportation accident. Because strict packaging requirements are used in the shipment of radioactive materials, accidental spills or releases of these substances seldom occur. Very few emergency responders have ever had to deal with transportation accidents involving radioactive materials, and these accidents will continue to be rare occurrences.

Nevertheless, it is prudent for you, as an emergency responder, to know your role in responding to such an accident should one occur in your community.

Radiation is energy that comes from a source and travels through some material or through space. Light, heat and sound are types of radiation. The kind of radiation discussed in this presentation is called ionizing radiation because it can produce charged particles (ions) in matter.

Ionizing radiation is produced by unstable atoms. Unstable atoms differ from stable atoms because they have an excess of energy or mass or both. Unstable atoms are said to be radioactive. In order to reach stability, these atoms give off, or emit, the excess energy or mass. These emissions are called radiation. The kinds of radiation are electromagnetic (like light) and particulate (i.e., mass given off with the energy of motion). Gamma radiation and X-rays are examples of electromagnetic radiation. Beta and alpha radiation are examples of particulate radiation. Ionizing radiation can also be produced by devices such as X-ray machines.

Radiation cannot be detected by human senses. A variety of instruments are available for detecting and measuring radiation. Regardless of where or how an accident involving radiation happens, three types of radiation-induced injury can occur: external irradiation, contamination with radioactive materials, and incorporation of radioactive material into body cells, tissues, or organs.

Types of radiation exposure include:

— *External Irradiation*: External irradiation occurs when all or part of the body is exposed to penetrating radiation from an external source. During exposure this radiation can be absorbed by the body or it can pass completely through. A similar thing occurs during an ordinary chest x-ray. Following external exposure, an individual is not radioactive and can be treated like any other patient.

— *Contamination*: The second type of radiation injury involves contamination with radioactive materials. Contamination means that radioactive materials in the form of gases, liquids, or solids are released into the environment and contaminate people externally, internally, or both. An external surface of the body, such as the skin, can become contaminated, and if radioactive materials get inside the body through the lungs, gut, or wounds, the contaminant can become deposited internally.

— *Incorporation*: The third type of radiation injury that can occur is incorporation of radioactive material. Incorporation refers to the uptake of radioactive materials by body cells, tissues, and target organs such as bone, liver, thyroid, or kidney. In general, radioactive materials are distributed throughout the body based upon their chemical properties. Incorporation cannot occur unless contamination has occurred

These three types of exposures can happen in combination and can be complicated by physical injury or illness. In such a case, serious medical problems always have priority over concerns about radiation, such as radiation monitoring, contamination control, and decontamination.

2

Natural Disasters: Causes and Consequences

A natural disaster is the consequence of a natural hazard (e.g. volcanic eruption, earthquake, or landslide) which affects human activities. Human vulnerability, exacerbated by the lack of planning or appropriate emergency management, leads to financial, environmental or human losses. The resulting loss depends on the capacity of the population to support or resist the disaster, and their resilience. This understanding is concentrated in the formulation: "disasters occur when hazards meet vulnerability".

EARTHQUAKE

Earthquake is one of the most destructive natural hazard. They may occur at any time of the year, day or night, with sudden impact and little warning. They can destroy buildings and infrastructure in seconds, killing or injuring the inhabitants. Earthquakes not only destroy the entire habitation but may de-stabilise the government, economy and social structure of the country. But what is an earthquake? It is the sudden shaking of the earth crust. The impact of an earthquake is sudden and there is hardly any warning, making it impossible to predict.

Cause of Earthquake

The earth's crust is a rocky layer of varying thickness ranging from a depth of about 10 kilometres under the sea to 65 kilometres under the continents. The crust is not one piece but consists of portions called 'plates' which vary in size from a few hundred to thousands of kilometres. The theory of plate tectonics' holds that the plates ride up on the more mobile mantle, and are driven by some yet unconfirmed mechanisms, perhaps thermal convection currents. When these plates contact each other, stress arises in the crust.

These stresses can be classified according to the type of movement along the plate's boundaries:

(a) pulling away from each other,

(b) pushing against one another and

(c) sliding sideways relative to each other.

All these movements are associated with earthquakes. The areas of stress at plate boundaries which release accumulated energy by slipping or rupturing are known as 'faults'. The theory of 'elasticity' says that the crust is continuously stressed by the movement of the tectonic plates; it eventually reaches a point of maximum supportable strain. A rupture then occurs along the fault and the rock rebounds under its own elastic stresses until the strain is relieved. The fault rupture generates vibration called seismic (from the Greek 'seismos' meaning shock or earthquake) waves, which radiates from the focus in all directions.

Characteristics

Earthquake vibrations occur in a variety of frequencies and velocities. The actual rupture process may last for a few seconds to as long as one minute for a major earthquake. The ground shaking is caused by 'body waves' and 'surface waves'.

Earthquakes can be of three types based on the focal depth:

— Deep: 300 to 700 kms from the earth surface

— Medium: 60 to 300 kms

— Shallow: Less than 60 kms

The deep focus earthquakes are rarely destructive because by the time the waves reach the surface the impact reduces. Shallow focus earthquakes are more common and are extremely damaging because of their proximity to the surface.

Measuring Earthquakes

Earthquakes can be described by the use of two distinctively different scales of measurement demonstrating magnitude and intensity. Earthquake magnitude or amount of energy released is determined by the use of a seismograph, which is an instrument that continuously records ground vibration. The scale was developed by a seismologist named Charles Richter. An earthquake with a magnitude 7.5 on the Richter scale releases 30 times the energy than one with 6.5 magnitudes. An earthquake of magnitude 3 is the smallest normally felt by humans. The largest earthquake that has been recorded with this system is 9.25.

The second type of scale, the earthquake intensity scale measures the effects of an earthquake where it occurs. The most widely used scale of this type was developed in 1902 by Mercalli an Italian seismologist. The scale was extended and modified to suit the modern times. It is called the Modified Mercalli Scale, which expresses the intensity of earthquake effect on people, structure and the earth's surface in values from I to XII. With an intensity of VI and below most of the people can feel the shake and there are cracks on the walls, but with an intensity of XII there is general panic with buildings collapsing totally and there is a total disruption in normal life.

— *Predictability*: Although some scientists claim ability to predict earthquakes, the methods are controversial. Accurate and exact predictions of such sudden incidents are still not possible.

Physical Damage

Damage occurs to human settlement, buildings, structures and infrastructure, especially bridges, elevated roads, railways, water towers, pipelines, electrical generating facilities. Aftershocks of an earthquake can cause much greater damage to already weakened structures.

Secondary effects include fires, dam failure and landslides which may block water ways and also cause flooding. Damage may occur to facilities using or manufacturing dangerous materials resulting in possible chemical spills. There may also be a break down of communication facilities. The effect of an earthquake is diverse. There are large number of casualties because of the poor engineering design of the buildings and close proximity of the people. About 95 per cent of the people who are killed or who are affected by the earthquake is because of the building collapse. There is also a huge loss to the public health system, transport and communication and water supply in the affected areas.

Distribution Pattern

India falls quite prominently on the 'Alpine—Himalayan Belt'. This belt is the line along which the Indian plate meets the Eurasian plate. This being a convergent plate, the Indian plate is thrusting underneath the Eurasian plate at a speed of 5 cm per year. The movement gives rise to tremendous stress which keeps accumulating in the rocks and is released from time to time in the form of earthquakes.

Table 2.1: List of Significant Earthquakes in India

Year	*Location*	*Magnitude of 6+*
1950	Arunachal Pradesh - China Border	8.5
1956	Anjar, Gujarat	7.0
1967	Koyna, Maharashtra	6.5
1975	Kinnaur, Himachal Pradesh	6.2
1988	Manipur - Myanmar Boarder	6.6
1988	Bihar - Nepal Border	6.4
1991	Uttarakhand - Uttar Pradesh Hills	6.0
1993	Latur - Maharashtra	6.3
1997	Jabalpur, Madhya Pradesh	6.0
1999	Chamoli, Uttar Pradesh	6.8
2001	Bhuj, Gujarat	6.9
2005	Muzaffarabad (Pakistan) Impact in Jammu & Kashmir	7.4

Risk Reduction Measures

— *Community preparedness*: Community preparedness is vital for mitigating earthquake impact. The most effective way to save you even in a slightest shaking is 'DROP, COVER and HOLD'.

— *Planning*: The Bureau of Indian Standards has published building codes and guidelines for safe construction of buildings against earthquakes. Before the buildings are constructed the building plans have to be checked by the Municipality, according to the laid down bylaws. Many existing lifeline buildings such as hospitals, schools and fire stations may not be built with earthquake safety measures. Their earthquake safety needs to be upgraded by retrofitting techniques.

Public education is educating the public on causes and characteristics of an earthquake and preparedness measures. It can be created through sensitisation and training programme for community, architects, engineers, builders, masons, teachers, government functionaries teachers and students.

— *Engineered structures:* Buildings need to be designed and constructed as per the building by laws to withstand ground shaking. Architectural and engineering inputs need to be put together to improve building design and construction practices. The soil type needs to be analysed before construction. Building structures on soft soil should be avoided.

TSUNAMI

The term Tsunami has been derived from a Japanese term Tsu meaning 'harbour' and nami meaning 'waves'. Tsunamis are popularly called tidal waves but they actually have nothing to do with the tides. These waves which often affect distant shores, originate by rapid displacement of water from the lake or the sea either by seismic activity, landslides, volcanic eruptions or large meteoroid impacts. What ever the cause may be sea water is displaced with a violent motion and swells up, ultimately surging over land with great destructive power. The effects of a tsunami can be unnoticeable or even destructive.

Causes of a Tsunami

The geological movements that cause tsunamis are produced in three major ways. The most common of these are fault movements on the sea floor, accompanied by an earth-quake. They release huge amount of energy and have the capacity to cross oceans. The degree of movement depends on how fast the earthquake occurs and how much water is displaced.

The second most common cause of the tsunami is a landslide either occurring under water or originating above the sea and then plunging into the water. The largest tsunami ever produced by a landslide was in Lituya Bay, Alaska 1958. The massive rock slide produced a wave that reached a high water mark of 50 - 150 metres above the shoreline.

The third major cause of tsunami is volcanic activity. The flank of a volcano located near the shore or under water may be uplifted or depressed similar to the action of a fault, or, the volcano may actually explode. In 1883, the violent explosion of the famous volcano, Krakotoa in Indonesia, produced tsunami measuring 40 meters which crushed upon Java and Sumatra. Over 36,000 people lost their lives in this tyrant waves.

General Characteristics

Tsunami differs from ordinary ocean waves, which are produced by wind blowing over water. The tsunamis travel much faster than ordinary waves. Compared to normal wave speed of 100 kilometres per hour, tsunami in the deep water of the ocean may travel the speed of a jet airplane - 800 kilometres per hour! And yet, in spite of their speed, tsunami increases the water height only 30-45 cm and often passes unnoticed by ships at sea. Contrary to the popular belief, the tsunami is not a single giant wave. It is possible for a tsunami to consist of ten or more waves which is then termed as 'tsunami wave train'. The waves follow each other 5 to 90 minutes apart. Tsunami normally causes flooding as a huge wall of water enters the main land.

There are two distinct types of tsunami warning:

(a) International tsunami warning systems, and

(b) Regional warning systems.

Tsunamis have occurred in all the oceans and in the Mediterranean Sea, but the great majority of them have occurred in the Pacific Ocean. Since scientists cannot exactly predict earthquakes, they also cannot exactly predict when a tsunami will be generated.

(a) *International Tsunami Warning Systems*: Shortly after the Hilo Tsunami, the Pacific Tsunami Warning System (PTWS) was developed with its operational center at the Pacific Tsunami Warning Center (PTWC) near Honolulu, Hawaii. The PTWC is able to alert countries several hours before the tsunami strikes. The warning includes predicted arrival time at selected coastal communities where the tsunami could travel in few hours. A tsunami watch is issued with subsequent arrival time to other geographic areas.

(b) *Regional Warning Systems* usually use seismic data about nearby earthquakes to determine if there is possible local threat of a tsunami. Such systems are capable enough to provide warnings to the general public in less than 15 minutes.

The day-to-day maintenance of the gauge is carried with the assistance from authorities of the ports. Apart from the tide gauge, tsunami can be detected with the help of radars. The 2004 Indian Ocean tsunami, recorded data from four radars and recorded the height of tsunami waves two hours after the earthquake. It should be noted that the satellites observations of the Indian Ocean tsunami would not have been of any use in delivering warnings, as the data took five hours to process and it was pure chance that the satellites were overhead at that time. However, in future it is possible that the space-based observation might play a direct role in tsunami warning.

Typical Adverse Effects

Local tsunami events or those less than 30 minutes from the source cause the majority of damage. The force of the water can raze everything in its path. It is normally the flooding affect of the tsunami that causes major destruction to the human settlements, roads and infrastructure thereby disrupting the normal functioning of the society.

Withdrawal of the tsunami causes major damage. As the waves withdraw towards the ocean they sweep out the foundations of the buildings, the beaches get destroyed and the houses carried out to sea. Damage to ports and airports may prevent importation of needed food and medical supplies. Apart from the physical damage, there is a huge impact on the public health system. Deaths mainly occur because of drowning as water inundates homes. Many people get washed away or crushed by the giant waves and some are crushed by the debris, causes.

There are very few evidences which show that tsunami flooding has caused large scale health problem. Availability of drinking water has always been a major problem in areas affected by a disaster. Sewage pipes may be damaged causing major sewage disposal problems. Open wells and other ground water may be contaminated by salt water and debris and sewage. Flooding in the locality may lead to crop loss, loss of livelihood like boats and nets, environmental degradation etc.

Distribution Pattern

Even though India has not faced frequent Tsunamis but there is a need to identify the areas that are generally affected by Tsunamis. The whole of the Indian coastal belt is prone to Tsunami.

Table 2.2: History of Tsunami's in India

Date	*Location*	*Impact*
1524	Near Dabhol, Maharashtra	Sufficient data not available
02 April 1762	Arakan Coast, Myanmar	Sufficient data not available
16 June 1819	Rann of Kachchh, Gujarat	Sufficient data not available
31 Oct. 1847	Great Nicobar Island	Sufficient data not available
31 Dece. 1881	An earthquake of 7.9 in the Richter scale in Car Nicobar Islands;	Entire east coast of India and Andaman & Nicobar Island 1m tsunamis were recorded at Chennai.
26 Aug. 1883	Explosion of the Krakatoa volcano in Indonesian.	East coast of India was affected; 2 m tsunamis were recorded at Chennai.
26 June 1941	An 8.1 Richter scale earthquake in the Andaman archipelago.	East coast of India was affected but no estimates of height of the tsunami is available
27 Nov. 1945	An 8.5 Richter scale earthquake at a distance of about 100km south of Karachi	West coast of India from north to Karwar was affected; 12 m tsunami was felt at Kandla.
26 Dec.2004	Banda Aceh, Indonesia; Tamil Nadu, Kerala, Andhra Pradesh, Andaman and Nicobar Islands, India; Sri Lanka; Thailand; Malaysia; Kenya; Tanzania	The East cost of India was affected. The waves measured around 10 m high killing more than 10,000 precious lives.

Table 2.2 shows incidents of tsunamis that have affected our country.

Risk Reduction Measures

While it is of course not possible to prevent a tsunami, in certain tsunami prone countries some measures have been taken to reduce the damage caused on shore. Japan has implemented an extensive programme of building tsunami walls of up to 4.5 m (13.5 ft) high in front of populated coastal areas. Other localities have built flood gates and channels to redirect the water from incoming tsunamis. However, their effectiveness has been questioned, as tsunamis are often higher than the barriers. For instance, the tsunami which hit the island of Hokkaido on July 12, 1993 created waves as much as 30 m (100 ft) tall - as high as a 10-story building. The port town of Aonae on Hokkaido was completely surrounded by a tsunami wall, but the waves washed right over the wall and destroyed all the wood-framed structures in the area. The wall may have succeeded in slowing down and moderating the height of the tsunami but it did not prevent major destruction and loss of life.

Some other systematic measures to protect coastlines against tsunamis include:

Site Planning and Land Management

Within the broader framework of a comprehensive plan, site planning determines the location, configuration, and density of development on particular sites and is, therefore, an important tool in reducing tsunami risk.

- The designation and zoning of tsunami hazard areas for such open-space uses as agriculture, parks and recreation, or natural hazard areas is recommended as the first land use planning strategy. This strategy is designed to keep development at minimum in hazard areas.
- In areas where it is not feasible to restrict land to open-space uses, other land use planning measures

can be used. These include strategically controlling the type of development and uses allowed in hazard areas, and avoiding high-value and high occupancy uses to the greatest degree possible.

— *Engineering structures*: Most of the habitation of the fishing community is seen in the coastal areas. The houses constructed by them are mainly of light weight materials without any engineering inputs. Therefore there is an urgent need to educate the community about the good construction practices that they should adopt such as:

 — *Site selection:* Avoid building or living in buildings within several hundred feet of the coastline as these areas are more likely to experience damage from tsunamis.

 — Construct the structure on a higher ground level with respect to mean sea level.

 — Elevate coastal homes: Most tsunami waves are less than 3 metres in height. Elevating house will help reduce damage to property from most tsunamis.

 — Construction of water breakers to reduce the velocity of waves.

 — Use of water and corrosion resistant materials for construction.

 — Construction of community halls at higher locations, which can act as shelters at the time of a disaster.

— *Flood management:* Flooding will result from a tsunami. Tsunami waves will flood the coastal areas. Flood mitigation measures could be incorporated.

CYCLONE

Cyclone is a region of low atmospheric pressure

surrounded by high atmospheric pressure resulting in swirling atmospheric disturbance accompanied by powerful winds blowing in anticlockwise direction in the Northern Hemisphere and in the clockwise direction in the Southern Hemisphere. They occur mainly in the tropical and temperate regions of the world.

General Characteristics

Cyclones in India are moderate in nature. Some of the general characteristics of a cyclone are:

1. Strong winds
2. Exceptional rain
3. Storm surge

Cyclones are generally accompanied by strong winds which cause a lot of destruction. In some cases it is accompanied by heavy downpour and also the rise in the sea which intrudes inland there by causing floods.

29th October 1999, Super-cyclone with wind speed of 260-300 km/hour hit the 140 kilometre coast of Orissa with a storm surge created in the Bay-of-Bengal with water level 9 metres higher than normal. The super storm travelled more than 250 km inland and within a period of 36 hrs ravaged more than 200 lakh hectares of land, devouring trees and vegetation, leaving behind a huge trail of destruction. The violent cyclone was merciless and broke the backbone of Orissa's economy and killed thousands and devastated millions.

The development of a cyclone covers three stages namely

(a) *Formation and initial development state*: Four atmospheric/ oceanic conditions are necessary for the formation of a cyclone namely: A warm sea temperature in excess of 26 degree centigrade, to a depth of 60 metres, which provides abundant water vapour in the air by evaporation.

- High relative humidity (degree to which the air is saturated by water vapour) of the atmosphere to a height of about 7000 metres, facilitates condensation of water vapour into droplets and clouds, releases heat energy and induces drop in pressure.
- Atmospheric instability (an above average decrease of temperature with altitude) encourages considerable vertical cumulus cloud convection when condensation of rising air occurs.
- A location of at least 4-5 latitude degrees from the Equator allow the influence of the force due to the earth's rotation (Coriolis force) to take effect in inducing cyclonic wind circulation around low pressure centres.

(b) *Fully matured*: The main feature of a fully mature tropical cyclone is a spiral pattern of highly turbulent giant cumulus thundercloud bands. These bands spiral inwards and form a dense highly active central cloud core which raps around a relatively calm zone. This is called the "eye" of a cyclone. The eye looks like a black hole or a dot surrounded by thick clouds. The outer circumference of the thick cloud is called the 'eye wall'.

(c) *Weakening or decay*: A tropical cyclone begins to weaken as soon as its source of warm moist air is abruptly cut off. This is possible when the cyclone hits the land, on the cyclone moves to a higher altitude or when there is the interference of another low pressure.

Depending on their track on the warm tropical sea and proximity to land a cyclone may last for less than 24 hours to more than 3 weeks. On an average the life cycle of a cyclone (a cyclone to complete these three stages mentioned above) takes six days. The longest cyclone is typhoon John which lasted for 31 days (August to September, 1994 in the north east and north west pacific basins).

Cyclones vary in frequency in various parts of the world. The 7516.6 kilometres long Indian coastline is the earth's most cyclone battered stretch of the world. Around 8 per cent of the total land area in India is prone to cyclones. About two-third of the cyclones that occur in the Indian coastline occur in the Bay of Bengal. The states which are generally affected in the east coast are West-Bengal, Orissa, Andhra Pradesh; Tamil Nadu and on the west coast Gujarat, Maharashtra, Goa, Karnataka and Kerala.

Warning

Low pressure and the development can be detected hours or days before it causes damage. The satellites track the movement of these cyclones based on which the people are evacuated from areas lively to be affected. It is difficult to predict the accuracy. Accurate landfall predictions can give only a few hours' notice to threatened population.

India has one of the best cyclone warning systems in the world. The India Meteorological Department (IMD) is the nodal department for wind detection, tracking and forecasting cyclones. Cyclone tracking is done through INSAT satellite. Cyclone warning is disseminated by several means such as satellite based disaster warning systems, radio, television, telephone, fax, high priority telegram, public announcements and bulletins in press. These warnings are disseminated to the general public, the fishing community especially those in the sea, port authorities, commercial aviation and the government machinery.

Elements at Risk

Strong winds, torrential rains and flooding cause a huge loss to life and property. The 1999 Super Cyclone of Orissa killed more than 10,000 precious lives with women and children greatly affected. Apart from loss to life there is a huge loss to infrastructures like houses built of mud, older buildings with weak walls, bridges, settlements in low lying areas.

Typical Adverse Effect

First, in a sudden, brief onslaught, high winds cause major damage to infrastructure and housing, in particular fragile constructions. They are generally followed by heavy rains and floods and, in flat coastal areas by storm surge riding on tidal waves and inundating the land over long distances of even upto 15 kilometre inland.

— *Physical damage:* Structures will be damaged or destroyed by the wind force, flooding and storm surge. Light pitched roofs of most structures especially the ones fitted on to industrial buildings will suffer severe damage.

— *Casualties and public heath:* Caused by flooding and flying elements, contamination of water supplies may lead to viral outbreaks, diarrhea, and malaria.

— *Water supplies:* Ground and pipe water supply may get contaminated by flood waters.

— *Crops and food supplies:* High winds and rains ruin the standing crop and food stock lying in low lying areas. Plantation type crops such as banana and coconut are extremely vulnerable. Salt from the sea water may get deposited on the agricultural land and increase the salinity. The loss of the crop may lead to acute food shortage.

— *Communication:* Severe disruption in the communication links as the wind may bring down the electricity and communication towers, telephone poles, telephone lines, antennas and satellite disk and broadcasting services. Transport lines (road and rail) may be curtailed, Lack of proper communication affects effective distribution of relief materials.

Risk Reduction Measures

— *Coastal belt plantation:* Green belt plantation along the coastal line in a scientific interweaving pattern can reduce the effect of the hazard. Providing a cover through green belt sustains less damage. Forests act as a wide buffer zone against strong winds and flash floods. Without the forest the cyclone travel freely inland. The lack of protective forest cover allows water to inundate large areas and cause destruction. With the loss of the forest cover each consecutive cyclone can penetrate further inland.

— *Hazard mapping:* Meteorological records of the wind speed and the directions give the probability of the winds in the region. Cyclones can be predicted several days in advance. The onset is extensive and often very destructive. Past records and paths can give the pattern of occurrence for particular wind speeds. A hazard map will illustrate the areas vulnerable to cyclone in any given year. It will be useful to estimate the severity of the cyclone and various damage intensities in the region. The map is prepared with data inputs of past climatological records, history of wind speed, frequency of flooding etc. Land use control designed so that least critical activities are placed in vulnerable areas. Location of settlements in the flood plains is at utmost risk. Siting of key facilities must be marked in the land use. Policies should be in place to regulate land use and building codes should be enforced.

— *Engineered structures:* Structures need to be built to withstand wind forces. Good site selection is also important. Majority of the buildings in coastal areas are built with locally available materials and have no engineering inputs. Good construction practice should be adopted such as:

  — Cyclonic wind storms inundate the coastal areas. It is advised to construct on stilts or on earth mound.

  — Houses can be strengthened to resist wind and flood damage. All elements holding the structures need to be properly anchored to resist the uplift or flying off of the objects. For example, avoid large overhangs of roofs, and the projections should be tied down.

  — A row of planted trees will act as a shield. It reduces the energy.

  — Buildings should be wind and water resistant.

  — Buildings storing food supplies must be protected against the winds and water.

  — Protect river embankments. Communication lines should be installed underground.

  — Provide strong halls for community shelter in vulnerable locations.

— *Flood management:* Torrential rains, strong wind and storm range leads to flooding in the cyclone affected areas. There are possibilities of landslides too. Flood mitigation measures could be incorporated.

— *Improving vegetation cover:* The roots of the plants

and trees keep the soil intact and prevent erosion and slow runoff to prevent or lessen flooding. The use of tree planted in rows will act as a windbreak. Coastal shelterbelt plantations can be developed to break severe wind speeds. It minimises devastating effects. The Orissa calamity has also highlighted the need for urgent measures like shelterbelt plantation along cyclone-prone coastal areas. Species chosen for this purpose should not only be able to withstand the impact of strong cyclonic winds, but also check soil erosion.

FLOOD

Flood is a state of high water level along a river channel or on the coast that leads to inundation of land, which is not usually submerged. Floods may happen gradually and also may take hours or even happen suddenly without any warning due to breach in the embankment, spill over, heavy rains etc.

There are different types of floods namely: flash flood, riverine flood, urban flood, etc. Flash floods can be defined as floods which occur within six hours of the beginning of heavy rainfall, and are usually associated with cloud bursts, storms and cyclones requiring rapid localised warnings and immediate response to reduce damage. Wireless network and telephone connections are used to monitor flood conditions. In case of flash floods, warnings for timely evacuation may not always be possible.

Causes

There are several causes of floods and differ from region to region. The causes may vary from a rural area to an urban area. Some of the major causes are:

(*a*) Heavy rainfall.

(*b*) Heavy siltation of the river bed reduces the water carrying capacity of the rivers/stream.

(*c*) Blockage in the drains lead to flooding of the area.

(*d*) Landslides blocking the flow of the stream.

(*e*) Construction of dams and reservoirs.

(*f*) In areas prone to cyclone, strong winds accompanied by heavy down pour along with storm surge leads to flooding.

Typical Adverse Effects

The most important consequence of floods is the loss of life and property. Structures like houses, bridges; roads etc. get damaged by the gushing water, landslides triggered on account of water getting saturated, boats and fishing nets get damaged. There is huge loss to life and livestock caused by drowning. Lack of proper drinking water facilities, contamination of water (well, ground water, piped water supply) leads to outbreak of epidemics, diarrhoea, viral infection, malaria and many other infectious diseases.

Flooding also leads to a large area of agricultural land getting inundated as a result there is a huge crop loss. This results in shortage of food, and animal fodder. Floods may also affect the soil characteristics. The land may be rendered infertile due to erosion of top layer or may turn saline if sea water floods the area.

Distributional Pattern

Floods occur in almost all the river basins of the country. The Vulnerability Atlas of India shows pictorially the areas liable to floods. Around 12 per cent (40 million hectare) of land in India is prone to floods.

Most of the flood affected areas lie in the Ganga basin, Brahmaputra basin (comprising of Barak, Tista,

Torsa, Subansiri, Sankosh, Dihang and Luhit), the northwestern river basin (comprising Jhelum, Chenab, Ravi, Sutlej, Beas and the Ghagra), peninsular river basin (Tapti, Narmada, Mahanadi, Baitarani, Godavari, krishna, Pennar and the Kaveri) and the coastal regions of Andhra Pradesh, Tamilnadu, orissa and Kerela. Assam, Uttar Pradesh, Bihar and Orissa are some of the states who have been severely prone to floods. Our country receives an annual rainfall of 1200 mm, 85% of which is concentrated in 3-4 months i.e., June to September. Due to the intense and periodic rain, most of the rivers of the country are fed with huge quantity of water, much beyond their carrying capacity.

Warning

Flood forecasting and warning has been highly developed in the past two decades. With the advancement of technology such as satellite and remote-sensing equipments flood waves can be tracked as the water level rises. Except for flash floods there is usually a reasonable warning period. Heavy precipitation will give sufficient warning of the coming river flood. High tides with high winds may indicate flooding in the coastal areas. Evacuation is possible with suitable monitoring and warning. Warning is issued by the Central Water Commission (CWC), Irrigation and Flood Control Department, and Water Resources Department. CWC maintains close liaison with the administrative and state engineering agencies, local civil authorities to communicate advance warning for appropriate mitigation and preparedness measures.

Risk Reduction Measures:

Mapping of the flood prone areas is a primary step involved in reducing the risk of the region. Historical records give the indication of the flood inundation areas and the period of occurrence and the extent of the coverage. Warning can be issued looking into the earlier marked heights of the water levels in case of potential threat. In the coastal areas the tide levels and the land characteristics will determine the submergence areas. Flood hazard mapping will give the proper indication of water flow during floods.

Land use control will reduce danger of life and property when waters inundate the floodplains and the coastal areas. The number of casualties is related to the population in the area at risk. In areas where people already have built their settlements, measures should be taken to relocate to better sites so as to reduce vulnerability. No major development should be permitted in the areas which are subjected to high flooding. Important facilities like hospitals, schools should be built in safe areas. In urban areas, water holding areas can be created like ponds, lakes or low-lying areas.

Construction of engineered structures in the flood plains and strengthening of structures to withstand flood forces and seepage. The buildings should be constructed on an elevated area. If necessary build on stilts or platform.

Flood Control aims to reduce flood damage. This can be done by decreasing the amount of runoff with the help of reforestation (to increase absorption could be a mitigation strategy in certain areas), protection of vegetation, clearing of debris from streams and other water holding areas, conservation of ponds and lakes etc. Flood Diversion include levees, embankments, dams and channel improvement. Dams can store water and can release water at a manageable rate. But failure of dams in earthquakes and operation of releasing the water can cause floods in the lower areas. Flood Proofing reduces the risk of damage. Measures include use of sand bags to keep flood water away, blocking or sealing of doors and windows of houses etc. Houses may be elevated by building on raised land. Buildings should be constructed away from water bodies.

Flood Management in India, systematic planning for flood management commenced with the Five Year Plans, particularly with the launching of National Programme of Flood Management in 1954. During the last fifty years, different methods of flood protection structural as well as nonstructural have been adopted in different states depending upon the nature of the problem and local conditions. Structural measures include storage reservoirs, flood embankments, drainage channels, antierosion works, channel improvement works, detention basins etc. and non-structural measures include flood forecasting, flood plain zoning, flood proofing, disaster preparedness etc. The flood management measures undertaken so far have provided reasonable degree of protection to an area of 15.81 million hectares through out the country.

DROUGHT

Drought is either absence or deficiency of rainfall from its normal pattern in a region for an extended period of time leading to general suffering in the society. It is interplay between demand that people place on natural supply of water and natural event that provides the water in a given geographical region. The state of Kerala which receives more than 3000 mm of rainfall every year is declared drought affected as it is insufficient to have two good crops. The more the imbalance in supply the higher is the drought.

Causes of Drought

Though drought is basically caused by deficit rainfall,

which is a meteorological phenomenon, it manifests into different spheres because of various vulnerability factors associated with them. Some of these factors are human induced. Though drought is a natural disaster, its effects are made worst in developing countries by over population, over grazing, deforestation, soil erosion, excessive use of ground and surface water for growing crops, loss of biodiversity.

General Characteristics

— *Types of droughts:* Drought proceeds in sequential manner. Its impacts are spread across different domains as listed below.

— *Meteorological drought:* Meteorological drought is simple absence/deficit of rainfall from the normal. It is the least severe form of drought and is often identified by sunny days and hot weather.

— *Hydrological drought:* Hydrological drought often leads to reduction of natural stream flows or ground water levels, plus stored water supplies. The main impact is on water resource systems.

— *Agricultural drought:* This form of drought occurs when moisture level in soil is insufficient to maintain average crop yields. Initial consequences are in the reduced seasonal output of crops and other related production. An extreme agricultural drought can lead to a famine, which is a prolonged shortage of food in a restricted region causing widespread disease and death from starvation.

Socio-economic drought

Socio-economic drought correlates the supply and demand of goods and services with the three above-mentioned types of drought. When the supply of some goods or services such as water and electricity are weather dependant then drought may cause shortages in supply of these economic goods.

Elements at Risk

In general, all those elements that are primarily dependent on water are most affected. It affects the rainfed crops and then slowly creeps into the irrigated crops. People who are dependent on agriculture and areas where the other livelihood opportunities are least developed are greatly affected. The herdsman, landless labourer, subsistence farmers, women, children and farm animals are the most vulnerable groups.

Typical Adverse Effects

Drought, different from any other natural disaster, does not cause any structural damages. As the meteorological drought turns into hydrological drought, the impacts start appearing first in agriculture which most dependant on the soil moisture. Irrigated areas are affected much later than the rainfed areas. However, regions surrounding perennial rivers tend to continue normal life even when drought conditions are prevailing around. The impacts slowly spread into social fabric as the availability of drinking water diminishes, reduction in energy production, ground water depletion, food shortage, health reduction and loss of life, increased poverty, reduced quality of life and social unrest leading to migration.

Distribution Pattern

- Around 68 per cent of India's total area is drought prone to drought.
- 315 out of a total of 725 Talukas in 99 districts are drought prone.
- 50 million people are annually affected by drought.

— In 2001 more than eight states suffered the impact of severe drought.

— In 2003 most parts of Rajasthan experienced the fourth consecutive year of drought.

Risk Reduction Measures

There are various mitigation strategies to cope up with drought.

1. *Public Awareness and education:* If the community is aware of the do's and don'ts, then half of the problem is solved. This includes awareness on the availability of safe drinking water, water conservation techniques, agricultural drought management strategies like crop contingency plans, construction of rain water harvesting structure. Awareness can be generated by the print, electronic and folk media.
2. *Drought Monitoring:* It is continuous observation of the rainfall situation, availability of water in the reservoirs, lakes, rivers etc and comparing with the existing water needs in various sectors of the society.
3. Water supply augmentation and conservation through rainwater harvesting in houses and farmers' fields increases the content of water available. Water harvesting by either allowing the runoff water from all the fields to a common point (e.g. Farm ponds) or allowing it to infiltrate into the soil where it has fallen (in situ) (e.g. contour bunds, contour cultivation, raised bed planting etc) helps increase water availability for sustained agricultural production.
4. Expansion of irrigation facilities reduces the drought vulnerability. Land use based on its

capability helps in optimum use of land and water and can avoid the undue demand created due to their misuse.

5. Livelihood planning identifies those livelihoods which are least affected by the drought. Some of such livelihoods include increased off-farm employment opportunities, collection of non-timber forest produce from the community forests, raising goats, carpentry etc.
6. *Drought planning:* the basic goal of drought planning is to improve the effectiveness of preparedness and response efforts by enhancing monitoring, mitigation and response measures.
7. Planning would help in effective coordination among state and national agencies in dealing with the drought. Components of drought plan include establishing drought taskforce which is a team of specialists who can advise the government in taking decision to deal with drought situation, establishing coordination mechanism among various agencies which deal with the droughts, providing crop insurance schemes to the farmers to cope with the drought related crop losses, and public awareness generation.

LANDSLIDE

The term 'landslide' includes all varieties of mass movements of hill slopes and can be defined as the downward and outward movement of slope forming materials composed of rocks, soils, artificial fills or combination of all these materials along surfaces of separation by falling, sliding and flowing, either slowly or quickly from one place to another. Although the landslides are primarily associated with mountainous terrains, these can also occur in areas where an activity such as surface excavations for highways, buildings and open pit mines takes place. They often take place in conjunction with earthquakes, floods and volcanoes. At times, prolonged rainfall causing landslide may block the flow of river for quite some time.

Causes of Landslide

There are several causes of landslide. Some of the major causes are as follows:

1. *Geological Weak material*: Weakness in the composition and structure of rock or soil may also cause landslides.
2. *Erosion*: Erosion of slope toe due to cutting down of vegetation, construction of roads might increase the vulnerability of the terrain to slide down.
3. *Intense rainfall*: Storms that produce intense rainfall for periods as short as several hours or have a more moderate intensity lasting several days have triggered abundant landslides. Heavy melting of snow in the hilly terrains also results in landslide.
4. *Human Excavation* of slope and its toe, loading of slope/toe, draw down in reservoir, mining, deforestation, irrigation, vibration/blast, Water leakage from services.
5. *Earthquake shaking* has triggered landslides in many different topographic and geologic settings. Rock falls, soil slides and rockslides from steep slopes involving relatively thin or shallow dis-aggregated soils or rock, or both have been the most abundant types of landslides triggered by historical earthquakes.
6. *Volcanic eruption* Deposition of loose volcanic ash on hillsides commonly is followed by accelerated erosion and frequent mud or debris flows triggered by intense rainfall.

Type of Landslides

The common types of landslides are described below:

— *Falls*: Abrupt movements of materials that become detached from steep slopes or cliffs, moving by free-fall, bouncing, and rolling.

— *Flows*: General term including many types of mass movement, such as debris flow, debris avalanche, lahar, and mudflow.

— *Creep*: Slow, steady downslope movement of soil or rock, often indicated by curved tree trunks, bent fences or retaining walls, tilted poles or fences.

— *Debris flow:* Rapid mass movement in which loose soils, rocks, and organic matter combine with entrained air and water to form slurry that then flows down slope, usually associated with steep gullies.

— *Debris avalanche:* A variety of very rapid to extremely rapid debris flow.

— *Lahar:* Mudflow or debris flow that originates on the slope of a volcano, usually triggered by heavy rainfall eroding volcanic deposits, sudden melting of snow and ice due to heat from volcanic vents, or the breakout of water from glaciers, crater lakes or lakes dammed by volcanic eruptions.

— *Mudflow:* Rapidly flowing mass of wet material that contains at least 50 percent sand, silt, and clay-sized particles.

— *Lateral spreads:* Often occur on very gentle slopes and result in nearly horizontal movement of earth materials. Lateral spreads usually are caused by liquefaction, where saturated sediments (usually sands and silts) are transformed from a solid into a liquefied state, usually triggered by an earthquake.

- *Slides:* Many types of mass movement are included in the general term "landslide." The two major types of landslides are rotational slides and translational landslides.
- *Topple:* A block of rock that tilts or rotates forward and falls, bounces, or rolls down the slope.

Adverse Effects

The most common elements at risk are the settlements built on the steep slopes, built at the toe and those built at the mouth of the streams emerging from the mountain valley. All those buildings constructed without appropriate foundation for a given soil and in sloppy areas are also at risk. Roads, communication lines are vulnerable.

Distributional Pattern

Landslides constitute a major natural hazard in our country, which accounts for considerable loss of life and damage to communication routes, human settlements, agricultural fields and forest lands. The Indian subcontinent, with diverse physiographic, seismic, tectonic and climatological conditions is subjected to varying degree of landslide hazards; the Himalayas including Northeastern mountains ranges being the worst affected, followed by a section of Western Ghats and the Vindhyas. Removal of vegetation and toe erosion have also triggered slides. Torrential rainfall on the deforested slopes is the main factor in the Peninsular India namely in Western Ghat and Nilgiris. Human intervention by way of slope modification has added to this effect.

One of the worst tragedies took place at Malpa Uttarkhand (UP) on 11th and 17th August 1998 when nearly 380 people were killed when massive landslides washed away the entire village. This included 60 pilgrims going to Lake Mansarovar in Tibet. Consequently various land management measures have been initiated as mitigation measures.

Risk Reduction Measures

Hazard mapping locates areas prone to slope failures. This will help to avoid building settlements in such areas. These maps will also serve as a tool for mitigation planning. Land use practices such as:

— Areas covered by degraded natural vegetation in upper slopes are to be afforested with suitable species. Existing patches of natural vegetation (forest and natural grass land) in good condition, should be preserved.

— Any developmental activity initiated in the area should be taken up only after a detailed study of the region has been carried out.

— In construction of roads, irrigation canals etc. proper care is to be taken to avoid blockage of natural drainage.

— Total avoidance of settlement in the risk zone should be made mandatory.

— Relocate settlements and infrastructure that fall in the possible path of the landslide.

— No construction of buildings in areas beyond a certain degree of slope.

Retaining

Walls can be built to stop land from slipping (these walls are commonly seen along roads in hill stations). These are constructed to prevent smaller sized and secondary landslides that often occur along the toe portion of the larger landslides.

Surface Drainage Control Works

The surface drainage control works are implemented to control the movement of landslides accompanied by infiltration of rain water and spring flows. Engineered structures with strong foundations can withstand or take the ground movement forces. Underground installations (pipes, cables, etc.) should be made flexible to move in order to withstand forces caused by the landslide.

Increasing vegetation cover is the cheapest and most effective way of arresting landslides. This helps to bind the top layer of the soil with layers below, while preventing excessive run-off and soil erosion. Insurance will assist individuals whose homes are likely to be damaged by landslides or by any other natural hazards.

3

Nature and Scope of Disaster Management

SCOPE OF DISASTER MANAGEMENT

The term "disaster management" encompasses the complete realm of disaster-related activities. Traditionally people tend to think of disaster management only in terms of the post-disaster actions taken by relief and reconstruction officials; yet disaster management covers a much broader scope, and many modern disaster managers may find themselves far more involved in pre-disaster activities than in post-disaster response. This is because many persons who work in the development field, or who plan routine economic, urban, regional or agricultural development projects, have disaster management responsibilities. For example, housing specialists planning a low-income housing project in a disaster-prone area have the opportunity (and an obligation) to mitigate the impact of a future disaster if the houses incorporate disasterresistant construction technologies. In the same manner, agricultural development projects must be planned in such a way that they help stem environmental degradation and thus lower the farmer's vulnerability to losses from droughts, floods, cyclones, or other natural hazards. In fact, in dealing with natural hazards, the vast majority of disaster management activities are related to development projects; only a small portion are related to emergency response.

Objectives of Disaster Management

The objectives of disaster management are:

— to reduce or avoid the human, physical, and economic losses suffered by individuals, by the society, and by the country at large.

— to reduce personal suffering.

— to speed recovery.

When assisting refugees or displaced persons, a fourth objective is to provide protection to victims or persons whose lives or property are threatened by armed conflict, tribal animosity, religious persecutions, etc. The University of Wisconsin Disaster Management Programme defines "protection" as intervention by governments, international organisations, or private relief organisations to protect persons threatened by armed conflict. Intervention for refugees or displaced persons may include provision of sanctuary or a means of escape from conflict, and emergency support to victims threatened by disease, starvation, and exposure to the environmental elements.

ROLE OF DISASTER MANAGERS

The term "disaster manager" is applied to a person who has responsibility for planning and managing pre- and/or post-disaster activities. Disaster managers may be found in a variety of positions in many different types of agencies. The most prominent disaster managers are the personnel in governmental disaster preparedness agencies, national emergency or relief agencies, national reconstruction agencies, and emergency service agencies, departments or ministries. All require disaster management specialists.

Municipal or provincial governments often have disaster managers. Large cities will often have a director of emergency services; and persons in public health departments, police departments, or public works departments may be assigned additional responsibilities in emergency management.

Inter-governmental organisations often have specialised disaster or emergency management agencies. For example, the United Nations Disaster Relief Office (UNDRO) provides a wide variety of emergency management services to member governments. The United Nations High Commissioner for Refugees (UNHCR) and the United Nations Relief and Works Agency (UNRWA) provide specialised assistance to refugees. Even within the non-disaster agencies of the United Nations, there are often special emergency management offices. Examples include UNICEF, which has an Emergency Unit; the World Health Organisation, which has a Director of Emergency Relief Operations; and the Pan American Health Organisation (a regional office of WHO), which has an Emergency Preparedness and Disaster Relief Coordination office that focuses specifically on the Americas. The World Food Programme also has a special Office for Emergency Relief.

Some nongovernmental organisations, both at the local level and at the international level, are specifically organised to provide emergency services. The most prominent of these are National Red Cross and Red Crescent Societies, the League of Red Cross and Red Crescent Societies, and the International Committee of the Red Cross. There are also hundreds of other private relief organisations throughout the world organised to provide specialised assistance to victims. These agencies range in size and scope from small, local ambulance corps to large U.N. agencies with scores of staff and multi-million dollar budgets.

Many non-governmental development organisations (NGOs) have disaster specialists on their staffs. This is in recognition of the fact that disasters often occur where development agencies have normal programmes, and they cannot avoid becoming involved in post-disaster activities. This is also because of the frequency in which NGO's are called on to assist disaster victims. The specialists help to develop disaster plans for their organisations and to manage post-disaster operations.

Disaster management specialists can also be found outside of the systems specifically oriented towards disaster management or relief. Government ministries, such as agriculture, forestry, public health, defence, and public works, will often have major departments or key personnel assigned to disaster management or mitigation roles. It is common, for instance, to find a public works department employee who has assigned responsibilities for flood control activities. To be effective, that person must exercise responsibility not only in flood fighting but also inland use, settlement planning and evacuation. Thus, the effective disaster manager must have input into a variety of activities.

Many people who serve in critical roles provide useful services in disaster management. While they are not considered disaster managers per se, their technological knowledge and skills and especially their experience warrant recognition of their potential contribution and function in disaster management. The examples are myriad: city and regional planners, watershed management and water resource development specialists, flood control engineers and specialists, code enforcement officials, public health specialists, doctors and nurses, dietitians and nutritionists, economic and agricultural development specialists, social scientists and welfare specialists, clergy and religious/ecumenical personnel, structural engineers, architects, reforestation and range land management specialists, firefighters, police, and development workers in general.

Although the above typically serve as the decision makers, other specialists often have an impact on disaster management decisions. These specialists include representatives from civic groups, academia, and the media, persons from research institutions focusing on disasters or disaster consequences, disaster management consultants, directors of development agencies, city managers, and other government officials.

In order to be successful, a disaster manager must have abroad base of knowledge in many different subjects and the ability to blend this knowledge into workable coordinated programmes to meet the needs of those affected by disaster. A disaster manager must deal with six distinct sets of activities in order to affect successfully the course of events related to disasters. Known as the elements of disaster management, these include risk management, loss management, control of events, equity of assistance, resource management, and impact reduction.

Risk Management

Risk management consists of identifying threats (hazards likely to occur), determining their probability of occurrence, estimating what the impact of the threat might be to the communities at risk, determining measures that can reduce the risk, and taking action to reduce the threat.

In natural disasters, risk management includes:

- hazard mapping
- vulnerability mapping
- estimation of potential losses, which can include:
  - losses of housing and physical structures
  - agricultural losses
  - economic losses
  - losses to physical infrastructure (such as roads, bridges, electric lines, etc.)
- development of appropriate disaster prevention and mitigation strategies.

Risk management is accomplished by lessening the effects of the natural hazard or by taking actions in normal development projects that will reduce the risks to an acceptable level. For example, if flooding is determined to be a major risk, the risk can be reduced by physical measures such as dams, flood control embankments, or channelling of the streams. Risk can also be reduced by moving threatened communities from flood plains and/or restricting economic activities in the flood zone to those that could absorb flood losses (such as forestry or agriculture).

Loss Management

Losses in a disaster include human, structural, and economic losses. Loss management addresses each of these through both pre- and post-disaster actions designed to keep losses to a minimum. The most effective loss management activities occur prior to the disaster and are focused on reducing the society's vulnerability to the disaster. Actions include:

- improving the resistance of buildings and physical structures in the event of disaster

— providing improved safety for the occupants of buildings or settlements situated in hazardous areas

— increasing and/or diversifying the network of social support (or coping) mechanisms available to victims and communities in threatened areas.

Post-disaster loss management focuses on improving the response and broadening the range of support given to victims. This includes facilitating relief delivery and stimulating a rapid recovery. These are accomplished through emergency preparedness, which consists of (1) the estimation of post-disaster needs and development of approaches and programmes to speed relief, response, warning and evacuation of persons known to be at risk from an immediate threat, (2) the provision of emergency assistance to help reduce the impact of losses, and (3) reconstruction, to lessen the economic burden of long-term recovery.

Disaster preparedness refers to a broader range of activities, such as establishing emergency policies, developing evacuation plans, designating emergency shelters, and developing methods for rapid assessment of pre-positioning supplies. Materials planning emergency services, training and drills for emergency staff, training seminars and courses, and broad campaigns of public awareness aimed at preparing communities for the onset of a disaster are other aspects of preparedness.

Another means of improving response is to expand or diversify the portfolio of assistance given to the disaster victims. Shelter, water, food, medicine, and clothing are usually considered as the normal emergency response. The potential range of assistance is in fact much broader. It should include economic assistance, family re-unification, assistance to small businesses, rehabilitation of a community's public utilities, emergency assistance to farmers that enables them to harvest the remnants of crops, provision of food to livestock and draft animals, reduction of erosion caused by floods, social and psychological counselling, and literally hundreds of other activities.

Control of Events

The critical element of disaster management is the control of events during and after the emergency. It is important that disaster managers control a situation rather than respond to it. Control is maintained through the following measures:

— Anticipation of a disaster and the cause-and-effect relationships generated by each type of event.

— *Mitigation, or reduction, of the scope of a disaster*. Mitigation is the most important function in bringing disasters under control. The more that can be done to reduce the effects of disaster, the fewer problems a disaster manager will face in the aftermath.

— *Preparedness*. By reviewing the anticipated scope of a disaster, managers can plan adequate responses, develop organisational procedures, and prepare to meet the needs that are going to arise.

— *Accurate information collection and assessment*. Once a disaster has commenced, the manager needs to have reliable data upon which to base priorities and to guide response.

— *A balanced response*. Each type of disaster will require a different set of responses. The disaster manager must review the different strategies and approaches for meeting disaster needs and develop an appropriate mix of responses, so that all sectors of the community can be equitably assisted. More than one approach may be necessary in order to meet a variety of needs in the same sector.

— *Action*. Once a problem has been identified and a response strategy selected, the action must commence immediately. Appropriate action must be phased in a timely manner and undertaken before demands and needs escalate. Action delayed means lost opportunities and a lessening of control, which add to the suffering of the victims.

— *Leadership*. Disaster management should lead, rather than follow, public action. If programmes are timely, the first element of leadership is attained. Rapid response and timely aid give people hope and encourage them to take positive actions themselves to help meet their needs. A delayed response leads to confusion and frustration and may force disaster managers to choose alternative courses that are ultimately less desirable.

— *Discipline*. Disaster managers, disaster management systems and organisations, and all key personnel in the relief and disaster management system must operate in an orderly, precise, and disciplined manner. The appearance of discipline and self-assuredness will reassure the public and promote compliance. The success of a disaster manager relates directly to the leadership exercised and the ability to coordinate the actions required to bring order out of chaos.

Equity of Assistance

All disaster assistance should be provided in an equitable and fair manner. Assuring that all disaster victims are treated fairly and equally is an important element of disaster management. This is especially important at the national level when a variety of different relief agencies, each with different constituencies and demands by their management and donors, are trying to provide assistance. Doctrines of fairness must underlie uniform relief and reconstruction policies in order to insure that disaster victims receive fair treatment and obtain adequate access to the resources available.

Resource Management

Few disaster managers have adequate resources to meet all the competing needs and demands of a post-disaster environment. Thus, resource management becomes a critical element of disaster response. The disaster manager must be familiar with the resources available. He or she must know how to form them into a balanced package of assistance and how to maximise their use to the greatest advantage. For example, in the aftermath of a flood a relief agency may receive seeds that will enable 1,000 farmers to replant the crops that were destroyed by the flood. Yet disaster assessment surveys indicate that 2,000 farmers need replacement seeds. The manager who decides to give away all the seeds and reinvest the proceeds from the crop sales to purchase additional seeds can expand the number of persons serviced and thus maximise the contribution.

Impact Reduction

Disasters can have an impact far beyond the immediate human, physical, or economic losses. In a very real sense, disasters represent a loss of opportunity, not only to individuals, but also to entire societies. They can also be a serious setback to the country's entire development programme. The impact of the disaster on individuals and their society should be reduced to a minimum. For a nation struck by a disaster, this means managing the disaster in such a way that recovery is accomplished quickly and that the recovery efforts contribute to the overall development needs of the country and all its citizens.

DISASTERS IN HUMAN SETTLEMENTS

The principal disaster of this type is urban fire. When fires break out in Third World shantytowns they can have a devastating effect. Flimsy, wooden shanties packed closely together create conditions that allow the fires to spread quickly and burn virtually out of control. As unchecked urban growth continues throughout the Third World, this threat will grow even greater.

Disaster Victim

A victim is a person affected by a disaster. The term "victim" has many negative connotations. It provokes images of helplessness, of people who must be taken care of. For this reason, many agencies use substitute words such as "beneficiaries" or "recipients." Unfortunately, these terms do not adequately describe all the people affected and may not accurately depict the actions taking place. The term "survivors" could be used, but technically the word applies only to those who have escaped a life-threatening situation, whereas any individuals may be drastically affected by the consequences of a disaster even though they were not directly threatened by a loss of life. Victims are not helpless. They are capable of making intelligent choices. When allowance is made for their special need to cope with personal losses and to put personal affairs in order, they can participate effectively in all post-disaster activities. In fact, participation in constructive activity is one of the most effective means of coping, and disaster victims are usually highly active and thoroughly dedicated relief workers. Furthermore, as local people, they are particularly well suited to deal with the needs of their communities.

While most countries, and international law, do not classify combatants as refugees, some countries and NGOs do. UNHCR and other humanitarian organisations may classify as refugees persecuted people, such as tribal or ethnic minorities, who desire to flee a country but who still remain in their homeland. This classification can provide them protection until they can be relocated to another country. Those Vietnamese under consideration for the Orderly Departure Programme of UNHCR furnish an example.

The term "displaced persons" also refers to people who are forced to leave their homes and homeland as a result of droughts and famines. The Ethiopians who migrated to Djibouti because of the 1984 drought were displaced persons. Several definitions of "refugee" illustrate the differences. UNHCR defines a refugee as any person who,

> "owing to a well founded fear of being persecuted for reasons of race, religion, nationality, membership of a particular social group or political opinion, is outside the country of his nationality and is unable or, owing to such fear, is unwilling to avail himself of the protection of that country; or who, not having a nationality and being outside the country of his former habitual residence as a result of such events, is unable or, owing to such fear, is unwilling to return to it."

In armed conflicts displaced persons and refugees are of special concern to disaster managers. Displaced persons are individuals and families forced to leave their homes because of the conflict, but who remain inside their country. Refugees are noncombatants who have sought (or are seeking) safety by leaving their homeland and entering another country. The laws regarding refugees and displaced persons are vague in many ways. For example, do persons who flee their homes because of extreme economic hardships coupled with human rights oppression qualify as refugees or as illegal immigrants?

Disaster Types

Disasters may be classified according to how rapidly they begin and how long they last. In this classification system are two types of disasters: rapid-onset or cataclysmic disasters, and longterm or continuing disasters.

Rapid-onset disasters include earthquakes, cyclones, floods and tsunamis (popularly know as "tidal waves"). Slow-onset, long- term or continuing disasters include civil wars, droughts and famines, and epidemics.

This type of classification is useful because the general approaches that are used to respond to the disasters in each category are very similar. For example, in supporting refugees and displaced persons, feeding programmes similar to those that are required for famine victims are used.

In a cataclysmic disaster, one large-scale event causes most of the damage and destruction. Following this event there may be a tremendous amount of suffering and chaos, and secondary disasters such as landslides may occur. Yet, things soon begin to improve. By contrast, in a long-term, continuing disaster the situation remains constant or may even deteriorate as time passes. In a cataclysmic disaster the damaged area is usually relatively small, while the area affected in a continuing disaster may be extremely large.

Phases of Disaster Response

The Preparatory Phase. The preparatory phase of disaster response includes all of the activities that help a society and the disaster agencies to prepare for a disaster event. Activities carried out in the preparatory phase include organisation, legislation, development of procedures, inventories of resources, and establishment of response plans. These activities are broadly classified as disaster prevention, mitigation and preparedness.

In general, disaster prevention is event-focused. In other words, the objective of prevention is to prevent the disaster from occurring. Disaster mitigation accepts the fact that some natural event may occur, but it tries to lessen the impact by improving the community's ability to absorb the impact with minimum damage or disruptive effect. Disaster preparedness assumes that a disaster will occur; it focuses on structuring the emergency response and on laying a framework for recovery.

Warning Phase. Preceding most disasters is a period of time during which it becomes obvious that something hazardous is going to happen. Certain specialists focus on trying to detect signs of a building threat. By monitoring events, they look for indicators that tell when, where, and what magnitude the event may be. This is known as prediction or forecasting. The objective is to provide disaster managers with enough information so they can give the people at risk adequate notice or warning to prepare for the disaster and, if necessary, to evacuate.

At the present time, warning is possible for droughts and famines, cyclones and most severe weather phenomena, volcanoes, large scale fires, and in some cases earthquakes. Work is also underway in refugee management to develop early warning techniques that will let relief agencies know of impending refugee crises.

Emergency Phase. This phase of disaster response involves actions that are necessary to save lives and reduce suffering. They include search-and-rescue, first aid, emergency medical assistance, and restoration of emergency communication and transportation networks.

Some disasters, also necessitate evacuation from areas still vulnerable to further disaster events and provision of temporary shelter, food, and water. Other actions taken during the emergency phase include initial disaster assessment and emergency repairs to critical facilities.

Rehabilitation (Or Transitional) Phase. The transitional phase is a time period when people begin to return to work, to repair infrastructure, damaged buildings and critical facilities, and to take other actions necessary to help the community to return to normal. During this phase, emotional recovery occurs as families and individuals regroup and try to put their lives back in order. In many ways, the rehabilitation period is the most difficult for the victims. Relief agencies must be sensitive to varying degrees of need and must provide appropriate forms of assistance. Emergency relief measures must be discontinued during this phase so that people can begin to regain their self-reliance.

Reconstruction Phase. The reconstruction phase of a disaster involves the physical reordering of the community and of the physical environment. During this period people reconstruct housing and other community facilities, and agriculture returns to normal. The actual time span is often very difficult to define. It may start fairly early and may last for many years.

TOOLS AND METHODS OF DISASTER MANAGEMENT

Disaster management uses a variety of different tools, programmes, and methodologies to lessen the impact of a disaster and to provide the managers with means of guiding relief and reconstruction activities.

Prevention and Mitigation Tools

The primary focus of disaster management should be to prevent disasters and/or to mitigate those that do happen. Disaster managers can generally use four sets of tools. They are:

— hazard management and vulnerability reduction
— economic diversification
— political intervention
— public awareness.

The first two apply exclusively to disasters caused by natural phenomena, while the latter are used to try to mitigate impending refugee situations.

As a general rule government, intergovernmental organisations, and the larger VOLAGS carry out hazard management programmes. This is because many of the hazard management activities involve vast areas and require large amounts of resources. At the community level, however, small agencies and communities can undertake a variety of activities with little outside assistance. Planting windbreaks and building flood embankments are examples of such activities.

The role of the disaster manager in hazard management is usually to insure that development plans and programmes incorporate hazard management activities. For example, a country's office of disaster preparedness may help make the various ministries aware of the flooding problem and may carry out studies in conjunction with other ministries. The actual management of a watershed to prevent or reduce flooding is usually the responsibility of river authorities, or of ministries of forests, agriculture, human settlements, and/or rural development. These activities are often carried out with the help of the central planning office and/or rural and urban planning departments.

The range of specific tools for mitigating environmental hazards are:

— planning
— building regulations, including zoning, building codes, performance standards, and improved urban design
— strategic development or investment of sites and services
— economic incentives
— housing education, i.e., the training of home builders to improve the quality and performance of housing
— code encouragement, i.e., the use of building inspectors to advise and encourage homeowners to utilise disaster-resistant construction techniques (rather than simply to enforce codes)
— financial incentives as an inducement to builders to use hazard- resistant construction techniques
— insurance
— environmental management, for example, reforestation and rangeland management in watersheds
— immunisation campaigns to reduce the threat of disease.

Planning Strategies

Various strategies that can mitigate the impacts of hazards can be adopted through normal planning. Among these are:

— Adjusting normal development programmes to reduce losses. For example, certain varieties of crops that are more wind- or flood-resistant can often be introduced in areas prone to floods or cyclones.

— Economic diversification. In regions where the principal or sole source of income is threatened, planners should attempt to diversify the economy and introduce economic activities that are less vulnerable, or not as vulnerable to the same types of disaster. Diversification is extremely important where economies are based on a single cash crop. Small island countries that depend on exporting bananas, palm oil, or other tropical agricultural products are vulnerable to extensive damage in a cyclone. Such countries could diversify into fishing, light manufacturing, or other activities, for example. Diversification will help protect the economy against natural disasters and also against unanticipated price fluctuations on the international market.

— Developing "disaster resistant" economic activities within a region. Some economic activities are relatively unaffected by certain types of disasters. For example, warehousing is more suitable than manufacturing for locating in flood plains. Coconut palms are more suitable than citrus or other fruit trees in cyclone-prone coastal areas. Efforts should be made to identify and to encourage the development of enterprises that are less vulnerable to the hazards.

Regulations

Planners can use three sets of regulatory controls for hazard management. These are land-use planning and zoning; building codes and performance standards; and land-use and building standards.

Conventional land-use controls regulate function, density, and location of activities, the rate of development, and limits of growth. "Zoning" may be defined as a division of land into districts or land-use zones; the prescription of regulations within these zones depends on how the zones are to be developed. Zoning ordinances are usually divided into broad land-use categories, such as agricultural, residential, industrial, and/or commercial uses. Sub-zones may include such designations as reforestation areas, range-land management zones, and watershed management zones.

Zoning has a broad function in the reduction of vulnerability, since vulnerable areas can be controlled or set aside for certain types of development. For example, a hazardous area can be zoned permanently for agricultural or recreational use, thus minimising concentrations of a population or a built environment on this site.

Land-use controls and regulations can be an effective tool for reducing vulnerability, but they are not a universal cure. Controls must be relevant to local conditions and must be formulated with a realistic assessment of the actual risk.

Building codes are used to control the built environment within an area. Economic concerns often dictate that hazardous areas be developed. To offset the threat and mitigate potential damages, building codes can be formulated to guide construction so that buildings and other man-made structures are as safe as possible.

Building codes and land-use zoning are often criticised as being ineffective in less developed countries, since enforcement is difficult and most growth is unregulated. Furthermore, codes and zoning are considered "passive" regulatory instruments; their enforcement often creates an adversary system between the public and the government. If development occurs in an area where it is not permitted, governments are usually powerless to reverse the situation. Enforcement activities may give rise to corrupt inspection officials who institute a system of bribery to overlook nonconforming uses or structures.

Because of these criticisms, planners have recently proposed an alternative that appears more workable in many of the developing countries. This is known as performance standard zoning and building regulation. In this approach, flexible standards are developed and adopted. They permit a variety of uses and construction as long as certain basic, minimal standards of safety and health are met. The standards usually permit people to use a variety of approaches to attain the desired standard. Rather than strictly enforcing the standard, the government makes a commitment to provide technical and planning assistance to persons in order to enable them to reach the highest standard possible. This type of approach is called an "active" approach. While it may be more expensive, a higher degree of compliance can usually be attained. Furthermore, governments become advocates and advisors rather than adversaries.

Strategic Investment

Planners are often able to encourage development away from hazardous areas by investing or creating a favourable environment for investment in less vulnerable regions or communities. This strategy is often difficult to implement in regional development. Most hazards are not site- or area-specific; they can threaten wide areas. For example, earthquake zones often extend for thousands of miles, and relocation of threatened settlements or enterprises is often not possible. Furthermore, hazards that occur infrequently are usually not considered in economic development planning.

Strategic investment has proven successful in agricultural sectors. For example, regional planning authorities in India have been successful in extending irrigation, land reclamation activities, and regional farm-to-market roads onto coastal plains that might otherwise have been developed with more intensive forms of economic activities. By developing the coastal plains with large, plantation agriculture relying on fewer labourers, the authorities have substantially mitigated human losses from hurricanes.

Economic Incentives

Governments are often able to extend a number of economic incentives to people and organisations in order to encourage development away from hazardous areas. Examples of incentives include provision of land, loans, grants, favourable credit, favourable taxation, technical assistance, or a combination of these.

In an effort to reduce human and agricultural losses, the government of Bangladesh recently initiated a programme to provide small plots of irrigated land to landless peasants; these persons normally worked as sharecroppers on hazardous floodplains in the lower Brahmaputra delta and on low-lying, offshore islands threatened by hurricanes and storm surges. Low-cost loans for initial land development were made available through cooperating private sector institutions, and relocation grants were provided by the government. Once people had arrived in the new areas, technical assistance for farming was provided by government agricultural extentionists.

Public Awareness and Education for Hazard Management

Effective hazard management requires an informed public, especially those at risk. In hazard management this is called public awareness. Public awareness campaigns disseminate information about the types of hazard, the effects of a hazard, the measures available to reduce the impact, and the actions to take when the hazard strikes.

Typical public awareness activities include:

- film and video programmes that illustrate and describe the hazard and the risk and demonstrate what can be done to prevent or mitigate losses.
- radio programmes.
- school curricula and booklets that include lessons and projects about hazard mitigation.
- comic books (perhaps based on the films or video programmes) made available for general distribution.
- posters placed around the community to act as a general reminder of the issues.
- presentations on the subject made to public groups or private organisations (e.g., neighbourhood councils).
- brochures and handouts distributed door-to-door or at public event, fairs, etc.
- features or articles in local media, especially periodicals.

It is crucial to promote disaster awareness in areas where risk and vulnerability are high and people are indifferent to potential hazards.

Public awareness activities can help motivate the public to initiate precautionary measures. Such activities can influence decision-making at all levels. However, public awareness will not be successful unless it is continuous and highly visible.

A public awareness programme for disaster mitigation describes or demonstrates techniques that can be taken to keep a disaster from happening. These can include cultivating droughtresistant food crops, making structural improvements to buildings to withstand the forces of earthquakes or high winds, and siting buildings or agricultural land out of floodplains.

Public awareness is also an important disaster preparedness tool. Preparedness awareness activities are designed to inform the public about what individuals can and should do to protect themselves and their property. Disaster preparedness activities naturally vary with each type of disaster. In the case of high winds, people would be encouraged to board up windows, batten down loose objects, etc. In the case of flooding, evacuation routes would be identified for the public. If a communicable disease epidemic threatens, information about its mode of transmission and means of control would be important.

Timing for a public awareness programme in disaster preparedness depends on the type of disaster. For predictable and seasonal hazards such as flooding and high winds, a programme of public awareness should be initiated immediately before and during the season. For slow-onset disasters (e.g., drought), implementation should begin as soon as there are indicators of its development. For non predictable events (e.g., earthquakes), issues of preparedness need to be brought continuously to the public's consciousness.

Economic Mitigation

The purpose of economic mitigation is to reduce the disaster's impact on the economy and on the economic well-being of the disaster victims. This is done by strengthening those sectors of the economy that are particularly vulnerable to disasters, by diversifying the economy, by introducing or expanding "disaster-resistant" economic activities, and by spreading or relocating economic activities to less vulnerable areas so that not all the principal enterprises would be affected at the same time. Insurance or other economic risk-spreading activities are also possible.

Economic mitigation uses the same general methodology employed to reduce physical losses. Once hazard mapping has been completed, planners identify those sectors of the economy that are vulnerable to disasters. This is done by relating risk to economic activities or means of production. First, the key elements of the economy and those that are not particularly vulnerable to disaster are identified. Often this is not difficult, especially for countries that have one-crop economies or only a few industries that earn foreign currency. Every economic activity is examined to determine if a hazard could affect a significant portion of that activity. This analysis is conducted on both the macro and micro levels. In other words, even though a flood may not have a significant economic impact on a country as a whole, it may have a major impact on a community or region.

Economic vulnerability determinations should consider other critical activities and installations. Energy facilities and systems are of prime concern, as are transportation networks, fuel distribution facilities, road systems, and financial institutions. Even though the means of production may not be affected by a disaster, the disruption of transportation networks can make difficult the marketing or distribution of goods. Economic diversification and insurance are the two primary economic mitigation measures. Diversification spreads the risk so that if a disaster occurs, the total losses in any one area or sector are acceptable. For many countries diversification can be a difficult choice. Small nations that are dependent upon one or two crops for their livelihood may find it politically and economically difficult to justify diversification simply on grounds of disaster mitigation.

In this case, long-term development choices come into play. The decision may ultimately rest more on political or economical factors than on disaster mitigation strategies.

Insurance can play a major role in mitigating disaster losses. Unfortunately, there are too few programmes currently available for low-income persons in the developing countries, although new programmes and alternative insurance schemes are being developed. In some cases governments and large economic institutions have found alternative ways of providing insurance to low-income people. For example, cooperatives can often be insured even though individual farmers who are members of the cooperative cannot. If a disaster occurs, the insurance pays the cooperative, which in turn divides the proceeds of the insurance among its members.

The indirect effect of insurance is also important to consider. Disaster claims paid for large institutions, facilities, installations, or structures can infuse much needed cash into the local economy. This can have a spin-off effect reflected in increased jobs, increased purchases and orders for local suppliers, and other economic boosts to the area affected by a disaster. Thus, even if it is not possible to insure low-income families and their houses, farms or business, the objective of disaster management should be to insure the maximum number of larger economic activities.

Adjusting On-Going Development Activities

Adjustment to on-going development programmes is a major way to address disaster mitigation. Many development projects have the potential to reduce either physical or economic vulnerability of families and communities. For example, housing programmes can incorporate, often at little or no additional cost, a variety of disasterresistant construction and planning techniques;

unfortunately these measures are frequently overlooked because the development programme planners are not aware of disaster mitigation opportunities. Thus, an important function of disaster management is to review and adjust normal development programmes so that they help mitigate or prevent future disasters. Areas of particular interest are:

— housing and urban development programmes (siting and construction).
— establishment of new settlements.
— forestry projects.
— agricultural development projects land reclamation.
— rangeland management.

Diversification and Expansion of the Social Support Network

The level of disorganisation that results from a disaster is an inverse function of the level of social organisation of the community. Societies with an overlapping complex of social organisations, both formal and informal, can more easily absorb a disaster and more quickly respond. In Third World poor communities, the network of social organisations is usually minimal; as a consequence, a disaster can have a far greater impact on the poor community.

Diversification of a community's social structure is an important mitigation measure. For the most part this can best be accomplished through extending normal development work in one of three ways. The first is institution building. Local organisations that serve as a means of coping with disasters or providing support to disaster victims should be identified and strengthened. A conscious effort to increase the organisations, capacities and skills can enhance their abilities to deal with crises.

The second activity is to increase the number of coping mechanisms within the community. By developing formal institutions and linking these groups to outside resources, communities can establish vehicles for intervention and assistance.

The third activity is to broaden the scope of service of local groups and to encourage activities that promote cooperation among different elements or groups within the society. Such cooperation can reduce the social impact of a disaster.

By increasing self-sufficiency and reliance on internal resources, agencies improve the ability of local people to cope with a disaster. This can be a mitigating factor and can help to speed recovery.

TECHNOLOGIES OF DISASTER MANAGEMENT

Disaster managers should be familiar with certain technologies or sets of information used in disaster management. Among the more important are mapping, interpretation of aerial photography, communications, information management, logistics and computer applications, epidemiology and preventive medicine.

Mapping

Disaster management relies heavily on the use of maps and mapping techniques for control of disasters and for managing response. At a minimum, disaster managers must be familiar with a variety of different types of maps including topographic maps, land-use maps, hazard maps, geologic maps, vegetation maps, population distribution maps, seismic maps, and hurricane tracking maps. Disaster managers must know how to read maps. They must also know how to plot information accurately on the maps and how to interpret trends through map reading.

The introduction of microcomputers to disaster management will increase the use of computer-generated maps. Schematic maps generated through computer graphics are being used to provide updated information about disaster situations as they develop. For example, these maps can be used to monitor flooding and guide a disaster manager who must decide when to evacuate certain areas. By monitoring the stream flow and water level at an upstream location, a disaster manager can map the expected flood zone and predict threatened areas, the extent of the flooding, and areas that should be evacuated on a priority basis. The manager can likewise determine where to focus flood control activities.

Computer-generated maps are used in risk analysis, vulnerability analysis, evacuation planning, flood monitoring, damage assessment, and reconstruction planning.

Aerial Photography and Remote Sensing

Aerial photography used wisely is a valuable tool for disaster managers. It can be an expensive tool if misused. Disaster managers must know how to interpret aerial photography and how to apply it to both pre-disaster planning and post-disaster response activities. Possible uses of aerial photography include hazard analysis and mapping, vulnerability analysis and mapping, disaster assessment, reconstruction planning and management.

Remote sensing is the acquisition of information about a subject that is at a distance from the information-gathering device. Weather radar, weather satellite, seismographs, sono buoys, and videotape are examples of remote sensing systems. Aerial photography is a form of remote sensing, but in disaster management the term generally refers to the use of satellites with imaging systems that produce a computer-generated image resembling a photograph and with other electronic monitoring devices. For example, meteorological satellites track hurricanes by remote sensing. The "picture" of the hurricane is a computer- generated image made by the satellite's sensors.

The use of remote sensing in disaster management is increasing. Pre-disaster uses include risk analysis and mapping; disaster warning, especially cyclone tracking, drought monitoring, volcanoes, large-scale fires and agricultural production; and disaster assessment, especially flood monitoring and assessment, estimation of crop and forestry damages, and monitoring of land-use changes in the aftermath of a disaster. Meteorological satellites monitor weather patterns, detect and track storm systems, and monitor frosts and floods.

Communications

Electronic communications are an important technology of disaster management. Electronic communications are used for coordination and control, assessment, reporting, monitoring and scheduling logistics, and re-unification and tracing separated families. A disaster manager must be familiar with communications equipment and their limitations. He or she must understand the effective use of communications networks both prior to and in the aftermath of a disaster.

A disaster manager must above all know how to communicate, what to communicate, and with whom to communicate, using the different technologies available. Electronic communications too often give disaster managers the impression that they can control a situation simply by communicating. The information that comes in through electronic communications can often overwhelm and/or misinform a manager. Thus the manager must be knowledgeable about the systems, but he or she must also know how to structure the communications systems. Structuring will allow rapid communication of vital information and accurate assessment of a developing situation.

Information Management

Disaster management is highly dependent on accurate information collection and interpretation. Disaster managers must therefore be familiar with how to collect, structure, and evaluate information in emergency situations. This is usually done by establishing an information management system. In recent years microcomputers have provided disaster managers with a new tool for structuring information and data and analysing information patterns and trends. Micro-computers are now routinely used for programme planning, project scheduling and monitoring, management of logistics, damage assessment, casualty management, communications, and cost accounting management.

Logistics

Every disaster manager eventually becomes involved in logistics. Therefore, he or she must be familiar with basic logistics planning, inventory management, warehousing and stock control procedures, materials distribution methods, and accounting procedures. Logistics planning can include, for example, evaluating the capability and capacity to move supplies through the relief system identifying bottlenecks and developing alternate solutions. Logistics planning in a country struck by a disaster might include the estimation of the capacity to receive supplies at air and sea ports and to unload the supplies and reload into trucks. It might include determining the sufficiency of trucks of the right size and type, and the availability of parts and fuel for the trucks. Other considerations might be adequate roads to the site of relief, adequate warehouses at collection points, and a distribution system with the administrative capability and the methods to deliver the goods to the final point of utilisation.

Epidemiology

Epidemiology is the branch of medicine that investigates the causes and control of epidemics. In relation to disasters epidemiology has come to mean the evaluation of all the causes of the occurrence or non-occurrence of a disease (and more broadly of the death and injuries) resulting from a disaster. Epidemiologic surveillance after disasters and refugee crises includes identification of diseases to include in the surveillance; the collection, interpretation and utilization of data; laboratory diagnosis of samples; development of policies and plans for a public health programme; and establishment of a programme for the control of communicable disease. The last two points coincide with programmes in environmental health management and preventive medicine.

Additional Technologies of Disaster Management

Many disaster managers become involved with disasters through their specialised job skills or through their work in a specific sector of the government or economy. For example, an engineer in a department of public works may need to know the technologies of road repair after flooding or landslides and of bridge repair after an earthquake. The following are other examples of skills or technologies for which special training may enhance the individual's disaster management capabilities.

Agriculture, production, and food systems and technologies that relate to disasters identify disasterresistant crops, methods of restoring crops damaged by disaster, restoration practices for soils damaged by a disaster, and alternative crops to replace quickly the losses from disasters. The last action will minimise dependence on outside food and economic aid.

Disaster assessment is the technique of evaluating the damage and the needs created by a disaster. Useful disaster management assessment identifies procedures for data collection and information dissemination; it also identifies priorities for relief assistance.

Refugee camp planning is essentially the discipline of town planning but with the added requirements of developing a human community environment under the crisis of emergency conditions. Such planning must take into account a volatile political reality and an uncertain future for the camp's residents. Additional aspects of refugee camp planning include the technologies of sanitation, security, circulation and transportation, water and food supply.

Meteorology is of use to disaster managers involved with warning, communication, search and rescue in areas subject to high winds, flooding, and even drought.

The following are additional specialised technologies that will further enhance a disaster manager's skills:

— personnel administration

— cost accounting

— government and non-profit accounting

— critical path techniques

— general geology

Such a list could be much longer, but the purpose of this section is to bring to the attention of the student the existence and the importance of these technologies. As stated at the outset of this course, a better trained and more knowledgeable disaster manager can contribute to more effective disaster services; he or she can ultimately reduce the disruption to society caused by natural and man-made disasters.

NATURAL DISASTER ASSISTANCE AND REFUGEE OPERATIONS

When most people think of disasters, they imagine voluntary agencies or the Red Cross or Fire Brigade etc. providing emergency relief materials and aid to disaster victims. While this image is, in part, correct, it depicts only a portion of the assistance that is provided and the manner in which it is delivered.

Government's Role

The ultimate responsibility for coping with natural disasters lies with the national government of the affected country. Responsibility for disaster mitigation is usually assigned to a government ministry. For example, mitigation activities for drought would normally be assigned to an agricultural ministry, while mitigation and preparedness activities for earthquakes would typically be assigned to a housing or public works ministry.

Preparedness planning is usually carried out by an inter ministerial committee or by a unit of government that specialises in planning and coordination. The latter may be a specially created preparedness group or it may be an existing planning group such as a central planning office. During an emergency the disaster preparedness authorities may assume responsibility for coordination of emergency activities, or a new emergency committee may be established. Depending on the type of disaster, however, operational responsibilities will again usually be assigned to one or more ministries, usually those with some degree of operational capacity or with special equipment required for the emergency period. For example, public works departments, which have trucks and engineering equipment, are often assigned lead responsibility during floods, while public health departments are usually assigned lead responsibility during famines or epidemics. During the post-emergency phases and especially during reconstruction, operational responsibility may be shifted to another government ministry or combination of ministries. If the disaster has been particularly destructive or widespread, special regional agencies may sometimes be formed with staff seconded from the normal ministries. These regional agencies tend to remain in existence for about one to five years. They are then disbanded and the personnel return to their former jobs.

Foreign Assistance Patterns

Donor governments and international voluntary organisations render foreign assistance when the disaster relief and recovery requirements exceed the resources available in the affected country. The assistance patterns vary according to the phase and the type of disaster. While many development agencies participate in development activities that might mitigate disasters, few would see this as their primary role. Likewise, few participate in disaster preparedness planning.

During the emergency phase, nongovernmental organisations often become prominent in dispensing emergency relief. This is because of their flexibility and inherent ability to respond quickly to an emergency. In general, non-governmental organisations should usually be regarded as specialised service agencies; that is, they have special skills or interests that are generally sector-focused. They usually provide assistance for only limited periods of time, primarily during the emergency and rehabilitation phase. Since their funding is dependent on public support and interest in a particular disaster. Voluntary agencies tend to work in person-to-person types of activities and generally prefer to do small-scale, short-term projects rather than long-term activities that require large capital expenditures. In order to make the most of scarce resources, governments often prefer to turn over large segments of humanitarian efforts to these agencies so that government resources can be channelled into longer term, and more expansive recovery activities. Because voluntary agencies work directly with the disaster victims, they tend to be highly visible. Yet their overall responsibilities are fairly limited.

During reconstruction, development agencies may also become involved. This is because many of the reconstruction activities involve development work, and many agencies recognise that the reconstruction period offers opportunities for advancing development goals.

Major foreign governments usually have a greater interest in disaster mitigation and preparedness than nongovernmental agencies. Most of the work in these activities has been stimulated by government donor agencies responsible for disaster aid. Foreign governments usually provide bilateral assistance directly to the host government and may provide technical assistance for planning, or financial assistance in implementation.

When a disaster occurs, foreign governments may provide assistance through several different methods. These include bilateral assistance to the government for general support or for specific projects and multilateral assistance through organisations such as the United Nations or various regional groups. They may also fund voluntary agencies to conduct specific projects.

The pattern of aid established during the emergency will usually carry over into reconstruction, but emphasis on voluntary agencies is generally replaced with more bilateral assistance directly to the government and its ministries. Technical assistance for project administration and planning is also a popular form of aid.

The United Nations system is another major source of international aid for disasters. The United Nations Development Programme (UNDP), the Food and Agricultural Organisation (FAO), and the United Nations Center for Housing and Human Settlements (HABITAT) are the principal U.N. agencies actively engaged in disaster-prevention programmes.

Preparedness activities fali under the domain of the United Nations Disaster Relief Office (UNDRO). UNDRO normally works through the UNDP resident representative (Resrep) in each country to provide planning assistance for disaster preparedness. This assistance is usually in the form of technical assistance and studies designed to help the government structure its emergency response.

During an emergency many different United Nations agencies may respond. UNDRO often sends a representative to help coordinate foreign donations. Acting on a government's request, UNDRO may stay on for several weeks to report on emergency needs and respond to those needs by external donors.

The United Nations specialised agencies may also respond with emergency assistance. UNICEF often initiates programmes for women and children, and in droughts the World Food Programme (WFP) provides emergency rations to augment available food supplies. UNHCR will sometimes assist the victims of natural disasters if they happen to be refugees or if drought victims are forced to leave their homeland in search of assistance. Most emergency assistance is provided as "project aid" by the U.N. agency using its own staff and locally hired personnel. The United Nations agencies have tremendous logistical capabilities and can undertake emergency projects on a vast scale.

During the post-emergency phases, the United Nations development agencies often take a lead role. The

FAO is usually very active in agricultural recovery activities while UNDP and HABITAT become involved in physical reconstruction of houses and basic infrastructure. Assistance in the later phases, however, is usually in the form of cash and technical assistance, not operational projects.

The Red Cross system (or Red Crescent in Moslem countries) can also bring many resources to bear in an emergency. The Red Cross/Red Crescent Society in each country is usually chartered by the government and given semi-official status. Each national society, in turn, belongs to the international League of Red Cross and Red Crescent Societies (LRCS) to which they can turn for additional foreign assistance should it be required. The Red Cross/Red Crescent is primarily concerned with emergency operations. The vast majority of their activities involve preparing for and responding to an emergency. Ideally, the national society will have many regional and local chapters, all of which have undergone some form of emergency training. In many cases, these are supported by a system of national emergency supplies that can be quickly augmented from international stockpiles maintained by the LRCS or obtained from its member societies through its international disaster appeals.

Because the primary focus is on emergency humanitarian assistance, most of the aid provided is "in kind" or materials. The LRCS also provides technical assistance to national societies in preparedness planning and emergency response management.

Worldwide, there are more than 1,000 different non-government, privately funded organisations that might respond to a disaster. These groups, known as private voluntary organisations (PVOs or VOLAGS for short) operate at both an international and local level to obtain funds and supplies for disaster victims. Most VOLAGS work on a person-to-person basis and focus their efforts on low-income families and communities. Some VOLAGS deal exclusively with disasters. These are considered "relief" organisations. Others focus more on development and work in disasters only when one strikes where the agency has a programme in operation.

Among the better known VOLAGS are CARE, Caritas, Catholic Relief Services, Church World Service, OXFAM, the Salvation Army, the various national organisations to Save the Children and Terre des Hommes, Medicins sans Frontieres, Christian Aid, Lutheran World Relief, and World Vision.

The resources they command give them an influential role in any operation in which they participate, and one or the other is involved in almost every country in the Third World.

Many NGOs at the local level provide assistance; and consortia, can often mobilise substantial resources. Some agencies have their own programmes administered by a professional staff, supplemented in disasters by volunteers. Others operate through local counterpart organisations, though in a few cases they do have their own programmes. Their interests are not restricted to any one sector. VOLAGS have entered housing, agriculture, small business, and many other fields, both in normal and in post-disaster times.

Refugee Operations

The patterns of assistance for refugee operations vary greatly from those of natural disasters. Under international protocol, the responsibility for the protection of refugees in the country of first asylum is assigned to the host country, but at their request this responsibility may be transferred to the United Nations High Commissioner for Refugees (UNHCR) or to another international organisation. Thus, in a refugee operation, the primary emphasis is usually on protection, assistance, and direct aid provided to the refugees by outside organisations. This is an important distinction. Rather than helping a local government to expand its capabilities to deal with a natural emergency, refugee operations try to ease the burden and responsibility of the host government. How much of this burden will be taken over by foreign assistance depends on many factors, especially on how long the refugees remain in the country of first asylum.

In reality, there is almost no pre-disaster planning for refugee operations. What little planning does take place usually occurs in the few days, or even hours, before the refugees arrive. The host government normally assigns a government task force, the military, or in some cases, an operational agency of the government, to oversee and coordinate relief operations.

Once the refugees begin crossing the border, the United Nations system, the League of Red Cross/Red Crescent Societies (LRCS) and/or the International Committee of the Red Cross (ICRC), an independent Swiss organisation established to deal with war victims, swing into action. The United Nations system is usually responsible for protection and coordination of assistance, while the LRCS or ICRC is responsible for humanitarian aid in the immediate vicinity of the conflict area or in a zone near the border. International voluntary agencies are usually available to assist in providing specialised services to the refugees. In many countries the U.N. agency becomes the coordinating agency for all international aid.

During the emergency period, voluntary agencies may work in a variety of roles. The U.N. has often requested VOLAGS with special skills or capabilities to assist in various field operations including processing and delivery of humanitarian assistance in refugee camps. UNHCR especially prefers to use VOLAGS as implementing partners in operational matters.

After the emergency, refugee support operations tend to become long, drawn out affairs. Many refugees remain in the country of first asylum for a decade or more. In some cases, host governments choose to allow the refugees to establish small settlements and farms so that they can help support themselves, but in many countries the refugees are forced to remain in camps while long-term, permanent solutions are sought. During the long interim period, referred to as the "maintenance phase," disaster managers have often found themselves working in what would otherwise be considered development work. Activities have included settlement planning, housing construction, water resource development, agricultural extension, and public health and nutrition work.

The primary objective of refugee assistance is to find a permanent or durable solution to the refugee's plight. The three solutions are voluntary repatriation (returning to their homeland), settlement in the country of first asylum, or resettlement in a third country. A key problem for disaster managers is how to provide assistance and protection to refugees in such a way that promotes, not hinders, the development of durable solutions.

Assistance Models

The term "victim" is non-specific. It encompasses everyone affected and obscures the reality that each disaster affects a specific group in a population more than others. Earthquakes affect people living in poor quality, non-engineered houses. In every type of disaster, specific groups of potential "primary victims" can be identified. The characteristics of these groups provide a key to determining the kind of assistance that is appropriate during each phase of a disaster. These characteristics also give an indication about how to deliver the assistance.

Disaster assistance deals with two types of aid: relief, which is designed to reduce suffering and replace losses; and long-term assistance, which might be called "change-related" aid. The objective of the latter is to encourage people to change their normal habits or practices in order to reduce their vulnerability to a disaster or to make sure that a disaster does not recur.

Knowledge of the characteristics of the victims enables us to plan for both types of assistance. Relief is the easiest. Droughts can again provide an example. Farmers, especially marginal, subsistence farmers, will be prominent primary victims. In an emergency they and their families will need food and alternative sources of income until they can replant and harvest a normal crop. Therefore, the relief programme must have a feeding component and a long-term assistance component; the latter, in the form of social services, will help the families find other means of supporting themselves until the emergency has passed and they can replant.

Knowing that primary victims will be farmers also helps us to plan disaster mitigation and reconstruction programmes. Both activities require that people change some aspect of their normal way of doing things. In the disaster context, change can be brought about in one of three ways: through public awareness, in other words providing people with information so that they will act on their own; through legal measures, i.e., forcing people to change by law; or through extension and education, i.e., demonstrating and teaching alternative methods and encouraging their implementation by means of a variety of services.

If we know that the target audience will consist of farmers, mitigation measures will involve changing crops, cropping patterns, or agricultural practices. This will require demonstrations, technical assistance, and extensive people-to-people contact. We also know that public awareness and legal methods will have little impact on changing agricultural patterns; therefore, the assistance model for mitigation and reconstruction must be based on extension and education.

Mitigating Measures of Refugee Crisis

Unfortunately, measures for mitigating refugee situations as they begin to occur are poorly developed and documented, and rather unsuccessful. The few measures that the international community has at its disposal are not well defined, and governments are often reluctant to exercise the ones that they do have. In the early 1980s, many humanitarian agencies began to talk of "early warning activities" and the development of political and humanitarian interventions that could possibly prevent or mitigate a crisis from escalating into a massive refugee situation. These discussions have thus far proven unfruitful, except to further emphasise the links between certain natural disasters and the political consequences that often follow-along with conflicts that lead to refugee migrations.

For refugee mitigation measures to be successful, a system of early warning must be in place to alert governments and humanitarian agencies of an impending crisis. The early warning would be based on indicators that a political situation could lead to armed conflict resulting in displaced persons and possibly in refugees seeking asylum in another country. Recent research has shown that a number of indicators can point to an impending crisis. Unfortunately, there is tremendous debate as to which interventions are then possible. The four most commonly discussed outside interventions are:

— *Political intervention by outside governments or intergovernmental organisations such as the United Nation:* Political interventions can range from military intervention to political or economic sanctions being taken against the country. Interventions are most often limited to expressions of concern by friendly nations.

— *Public opinion and moral persuasion*: Widespread public outcries against humanitarian abuses are considered to be the most effective tool for mitigating these abuses, although totalitarian governments have shown a remarkable ability to ignore world-wide opinion in many cases. However, a major public outcry against a particular situation may influence outside governments to take political or economic sanctions that could lead to resolution or mitigation of the situation.

— *Linking aid to human rights policies*: One measure sometimes used by western democracies is that of making economic or development assistance dependent upon the observance of human rights standards. In USA, this policy, first introduced by the Carter administration in the late 1970s, had mixed results. Most observers attribute this to an unequal application of the policy due to geopolitical considerations. It is likely, however, that this approach will continue to be advocated as an alternative to direct political intervention.

— *Internal interventions*: Thus far, most mitigation measures that have been discussed are those actions taken by governments or intergovernmental organisations outside the country where the situation is developing. There is often little that disaster managers can do inside the country. The measures are generally limited to moral persuasion and trying to influence public opinion. These are examples of non-governmental organisations within a country helping to reduce tensions and alleviating some of the problems. For example, religious organisations can often be effective mediators between parties in conflict. Relief organisations can frequently serve as a bridge between those seeking reconciliation. International organisations can often help reduce human rights abuses by placing large numbers of staff members in an area where abuses are occurring. These individuals serve as de facto observers and, by their presence, reduce human rights abuses. Nongovernmental organisations can often work in a partnership with the press to create a climate of accommodation and/or to help stem a growing crisis.

Phases of Refugee Relief Operations

The phases of refugee relief operations parallel in many ways the operations in natural disasters, but there are some significant differences.

Emergency: Preparedness is the set of activities taken by organisations to plan and prepare for reacting to a new refugee emergency. These preparations can and should meet any contingency, but they may also focus on a known situation that is predicted to develop into an emergency. Preparedness activities usually include organising, developing contingency plans, stockpiling emergency supplies, developing procedures, and training staff.

Monitoring And Early Warning is the process of keeping watch on current events in order to predict when political, economic, or social events may deteriorate to a point where information to diplomats may allow mediation before a crisis develops. Diplomats can also provide relief agencies with timely data that will facilitate the development of contingency plans specific to the area of concern.

Forward Planning is advanced planning carried out when an emergency is imminent, e.g., refugees are known to be displaced and moving toward a border. Some of the usual activities include preparations for protecting the refugees and granting them refugee status, as well as alerting agencies that will provide assistance.

Emergency Response encompasses the activities that occur immediately after the refugees arrive in the care of humanitarian agencies. Typically, emergency activities include protection and legal assistance; provision of health services-food, shelter, water, sanitation, and many other basic necessities for survival; and a variety of social services to people with special needs such as unaccompanied minors and widows with small children.

Maintenance refers to the services that are provided to refugees during the period after the emergency but before a permanent solution to their plight is developed. Maintenance operations may include tracing and family re-unification, general care and food distribution, a variety of social services such as education and cultural activities, and efforts to help the people to become as self sufficient as possible under the circumstances.

Durable (Permanent) Solution is the term used to describe collectively the three longterm solutions that resolve a refugee situation-voluntary repatriation, assimilation, and resettlement to a third country. In this phase, any number of activities can take place including transportation of the refugees, legal assistance, and provision of financial and material aid to the refugees to help them start their new lives. If the solution is repatriation or assimilation, the patterns of assistance often resemble reconstruction and development assistance given to the victims of natural disasters.

Evaluation occurs as a refugee operation ends or as a new phase begins. Evaluation should be carried out by every manager and key members of the staff. The results and lessons learned should become the basis for further emergency preparedness activities.

Preparedness Tools

The most important preparedness tool is the disaster plan and its various components. Every organisation that responds to a disaster should develop a plan that:

- — organises the response.
- — establishes an organisational structure for each phase of the disaster.
- — establishes objectives, priorities, and goals for the organisation.
- — assesses resources.

The development of the disaster plan permits disaster preparedness training, which is an equally important tool in preparedness.

Tools of Post-Disaster Management

A disaster manager uses a variety of tools to plan and manage disaster response. Most important of these are plans and procedures, policies, codes and standards, and standardised programmes or programme structures. The next four sections examine in detail these important tools.

Plans and Procedures

Plans and procedures are the most important tools of disaster management because they structure and guide emergency action. Plans are based on the premise that it is better to make your decisions long before a disaster strikes than in the aftermath of a disaster, when information is inaccurate and the situation is confusing and often unknown.

The primary types of plans and procedures are:

— *Disaster Plans:* These include preparedness plans, such as warning and evacuation plans; sheltering plans; disaster and needs assessment plans; search-and-rescue plans; and emergency services operations plans. Disaster plans are prepared on the basis of known risks, estimated impact areas, and predicted needs.

— *Contingency Plans:* Contingency plans are actions planned in anticipation that something unexpected might occur. For example, a government may determine that it can handle a disaster of a certain magnitude; it would then develop its plans accordingly. However, on the chance a larger magnitude disaster would outstrip its capacity to meet all the needs, a contingency plan for outside assistance might be developed.

— *Forward Planning:* This planning term concerns the development of specific plans to meet an immediate emergency. Forward planning is usually based on an early warning of an impending threat (for example, a warning from a meteorological department that a cyclone is likely to strike a certain community, or information that large numbers of refugees might soon seek asylum in another country). Forward planning usually involves the pre-positioning of emergency supplies and the preparation of emergency response services and resources for action.

— *Standard Operating Procedures (SOPS):* SOPs are developed within an organisation to provide standard responses to anticipated situations. The objective of a standard procedure is to help make the response routine and to eliminate the need for a lengthy decisionmaking process. If certain criteria are met, the response is triggered automatically. SOPs for specific disaster types in certain regions can often be compiled and presented in an emergency action manual. These manuals establish the tasks that must be carried out during each phase of an emergency and describe the procedure for accomplishing each in the proper sequence. They also structure the response so that everyone in the organisation knows what is expected and at what point each event should happen. They also structure the response so that each succeeding activity builds upon previous actions.

Policies

In providing assistance to disaster victims, organisations often propose many differing approaches and programmes. Different approaches often result in unequitable or unequal provision of materials and services. This can cause problems for the host government and for organisations with long-term commitments to the disaster-affected area.

Uniform disaster policies are one way to avoid these problems. Such policies provide a mechanism for shaping disaster mitigation and vulnerability reduction efforts as well as emergency response and reconstruction. They also provide a basis upon which programmes can be coordinated, and in some cases, integrated. Relief and reconstruction policies should ideally be set as part of the disaster preparedness process. However, if they do not exist at the time of a disaster, they should be established during the initial stages of emergency response.

Normally, the host government is responsible for the development and implementation of policies, but all major organisations, especially those that will be providing substantial relief aid, should participate in the process. Policies should be straightforward and concise. Simplified, brief policies increase the chances of voluntary compliance. Policies must be flexible, permitting relief agencies to adapt their programmes to the specific requirements of the communities in which they are working. The objective of policies is to guide action, not to dictate the precise nature and approach of all agencies. It is also important to incorporate a consistent development philosophy and goals into disaster policies.

Codes and Standards

Codes and standards are a primary disaster management tool used to mitigate losses and control reconstruction activities in certain sectors. In the housing sector, building codes or performance standards are used to set the minimum acceptable safety levels for houses and buildings. Specific codes and performance standards are also developed for hospitals, lifelines (water, sanitation, electrical and transportation systems), and critical facilities (government installations, communications installations, etc.).

Programme standards are used to establish the minimum levels of assistance and support that should be provided to disaster victims. In famine and refugee relief programmes, feeding standards are set according to nutritional requirements. For example, 1800 calories per person per day is considered the minimum average standard for food supplied to refugees or famine victims as part of a daily ration. Other standards may be applied to water supply, material assistance and services offered by relief agencies.

Standards are normally set by disaster managers in each relief agency, but there is a growing trend internationally to develop common, uniform standards for many of the social and humanitarian services offered universally.

Standardised Programme Structures

A relief agency will commonly develop a standard approach for responding to a recurring need in a specific type of disaster. Agencies trying a particular approach in one disaster will often develop a programme model that can be used in similar disasters in the same region. Some successful examples of standardised programmes are:

- supplementary feeding programmes
- shelter-to-housing programmes
- housing education programmes
- materials distribution programmes
- food-for-work programmes.

Some agencies feel that a standard programme will not meet all the needs of victims in different situations; yet they recognise the need for standardising the management of the disaster response. These agencies often develop standardised programme structures, which establish the key positions in an emergency programme, develop an organisation chart, and provide the preliminary resources necessary to initiate programmes. Sufficient authority is delegated to the programme staff to enable them to design and implement a programme tailored to the particular needs of the affected community. Standardised programme structures are workable only if the personnel are experienced and trained disaster managers.

Public Awareness

Post-disaster programmes can have an enormous impact

on a community. It is essential that they are planned to be effective and appropriate for the community, that they meet only the needs the community cannot meet for itself, and that the programme contribute to the development of the community. This frequently means that a programme's objectives should include the participation of the victims in the programme planning and design. The programme should have an educational component that will upgrade the level of knowledge in the community, to prevent or reduce a future disaster. The programme should also be tied to a long-range integrated development scheme.

Emergency Response

The primary purposes of public awareness activities during an emergency are to:

— alert the public

— instruct the public about the nature of the danger (repeating information from the preparedness stage)

— describe actions the public can take to protect their property and personal health, and warn people about what *not* to do

— explain what to do for food, shelter, medicine, or how to obtain assistance in locating missing persons.

The duration of the emergency period and its time of occurrence are functions of the type of disaster. The emergency period for an earthquake is usually the first week after the event. The period for high wind storms begins 48 hours before the storm strikes and lasts for approximately a week to 10 days afterward, depending on flooding. Slow-onset disasters such as droughts have an emergency period that continues until lives are no longer in danger. The timeframe for the emergency period is typically very compressed, and public awareness messages are usually coordinated with the civil defence or national emergency organisation. The most common media are the radio, newspapers, special printed bulletins, and posters.

Emergency public awareness programmes emphasise getting people to react. To do this, a well-planned and thoroughly developed system of getting timely messages out needs to be in place before the emergency occurs.

Awareness Activities for Recovery and Reconstruction

The general objective of public awareness during this period is to inform the victims how they, individually or collectively, can begin the process of recovery. Planning for these information activities should begin as soon as possible after the disaster.

The information needed includes advice about reconstruction of housing, sources of employment, or recovery in the agricultural sector. Recovery and reconstruction can and should begin immediately after the emergency has passed. Unfortunately this period is commonly characterised as one of false starts, mistakes, and waste. Accurate and timely information can help reduce delays.

The public awareness programme needs to have a similarly long perspective, and reconstruction information needs to be kept in the forefront of the public's attention. It is also important to remember that reconstruction and recovery programmes should encourage mitigation of future disasters.

4

Principles of Disaster Management

Disasters are among the most unique and urgent situations that humans are called upon to manage. Events and information are confusing, and authorities within the relief system are constantly faced with a need to make quick decisions. Management science offers the person in command a framework for making decisions and bringing these events under control. Delivery of relief and reconstruction aid can be improved substantially by detailed programme planning and thorough, sound programme management. A manager who applies to the situation both modern management principles and an understanding of disaster events can provide a well-balanced programme for a disaster's survivors.

The events of a disaster move rapidly and can be extremely traumatic for those who are unprepared. Disaster managers often do not get a second chance. If a decision is wrong, the manager and the victims must live with it. Therefore, it is extremely important that disaster managers thoroughly understand their role and responsibilities and be familiar with the tools of management.

Management consists of decision-making activities undertaken by one or more individuals to direct and coordinate the activities of other people in order to achieve results which could not be accomplished by any one person acting alone. Effective management focuses on group effort, various forms of coordination, and the manner of making decisions. Management is required whenever two or more persons combine their efforts and resources to accomplish a goal which neither can accomplish by acting alone. Coordination is necessary when the actions of group participants constitute parts of a total task. If one person acts alone to accomplish a task, no coordination may be required; but when that person delegates a part of the task to others, the individual efforts must be coordinated.

The principles of disaster management apply in both routine and crisis situations. Routine management relates to those activities that occur during non-crisis periods, such as disaster mitigation and disaster reconstruction. Crisis management applies to emergency operations and covers both the preparedness phase and the immediate post-disaster periods.

To neutralise the confusion of the emergency period, disaster management places heavy emphasis on advance planning. Advance planning activities, collectively called disaster preparedness, include strategic planning, contingency planning and forward planning.

- *Strategic Planning*: Strategic planning consists of preparing the organisation to respond to disaster threats in locations that are not specified and not immediately threatened.
- *Contingency Planning*: Contingency planning is site-specific and recognises that a disaster could occur at any time.

— *Forward Planning*: Forward planning occurs when a disaster is imminent and some details regarding the threat are known to the crisis manager.

A variety of different management systems have evolved to respond to different types of disasters, and no particular standard is used throughout the relief system. Until recently, most agencies utilised management models borrowed from military and/or business organisational models. These models usually consist of a pyramidal hierarchy of upper-level management, middle managers and field managers. As a general rule, upper and middle managers are concerned with managing the organisation and facilitating operations in the field. The field manager is responsible for the development of programmes that provide assistance directly to the people living in the disaster area.

In recent years, newer management models that allow greater sharing of decision making with disaster victims and give more rapid and responsive action have been developed and applied to disaster management.

Disaster management can be defined as the effective organisation, direction and utilisation of available counter-disaster resources. The role of an emergency manager can be divided into three parts: managing operations, managing people, and managing organisations.

— *Managing Operations*: Managing operations involves decision making, information management, problem-solving, project and programme planning, resource management, and monitoring.

— *Managing People*: Managing people includes leadership, organisation, personnel management, and personnel evaluation.

— *Managing Organisations*: Managing organisations refers to planning, control and direction, organisational development, quality/performance control, physical control, resource management, communications and evaluation.

MANAGEMENT OPERATIONS

As an organisation increases in size and complexity, its management adapts by becoming more specialised. In a relief agency, we may find top management (located at a central headquarters), middle management (represented by regional coordinators), field management (represented by field directors or managers at the local level), and various specialised managers handling personnel management, operations management, logistics, and financial management.

In the "one manager-many subordinates" type of organisation, the manager coordinates the work of subordinates. When the roles or activities of the organisation expand, the manager is confronted with certain activities, such as distribution of relief supplies or the task of supervising subordinates, to another person while continuing to be concerned with organisational tasks. Whatever the decision, the managerial process is now shared, specialised, and more complex.

Vertical Specialisation

Vertical specialisation is the creation of a chain of command and accountability. The chain of command is termed hierarchy because it results in a structured system of authority, with managers located at each point in a vertical chain. In this hierarchy it is possible to distinguish between field, middle, and top management.

— *Field-level managers*: Field-level managers coordinate the work activity of others who are not managers. Subordinates may be field workers, volunteers, disaster victims working for the agency, clerks or consultants, depending upon the particular tasks that the sub-unit must perform. Field-level managers coordinate the basic work of the organisation according to established plans and procedures. They are in daily or near-daily contact with their subordinates. They are ordinarily assigned to the task of field-level manager because of their ability to work with people-not only with their own subordinates but also with other field managers. The effectiveness of their efforts will depend as much, if not more, upon their human relations as upon their technical skills.

— *Middle managers*: Middle managers coordinate the activity of other managers; yet, like field-level managers, they are subject to the coordinative efforts of a superior. Middle managers coordinate the activity of a sub-unit of the organisation.

— *Top management*: Top management coordinates the activity of the entire organisation. They work through the middle managers. Unlike other managers, the top manager is accountable to no other manager, but instead to the suppliers of the resources utilised by the organisation (i.e., the donors). In non-governmental agencies, top management reports to a board of directors, which generally represents its major donors. In governmental agencies, top management must answer to the chief executive or to an oversight committee of the parliamentary body of government.

Virtually every major relief organisation uses a variation of this hierarchy. What differentiates the organisations is the amount of decision-making authority granted at each level. In some organisations, all major decisions are made at the top level. Senior staff are normally found only at the headquarters, while junior staff serve as field-level managers. In other organisations, the field-level managers are senior staff and all programme decisions are left to the field while financial and other organisational decisions are shared with top management. Middle-level managers serve as resource coordinators and facilitators. As a general rule, the latter organisation is usually more effective in an emergency. The terms used to identify managers at the various hierarchical levels differ from organisation to organisation.

Horizontal Specialisation

The completion of a task requires the completion of a sequence of interrelated activities. Middle managers are ordinarily responsible for the completion of major sub-tasks. As the sequence of activities is identified and as responsibility for completing each is assigned, the managerial process becomes horizontally specialised. Each manager is at the same level in the hierarchy, but each is responsible for completing a different part of the total task. Middle managers must integrate their own tasks and objectives with other middle managers.

Similarly, field-level management is usually responsible for managing sub-groups that are specialised horizontally. For example, a field director responsible for a reconstruction project may in turn have to rely on certain specialists on his/her staff to obtain the necessary resources and provide them for the project. Each of these staff members may manage parts of the project (e.g., logistics), yet within the organisation they would be of equal "rank." Successful completion of the tasks assigned to subordinates results in successful completion of the project.

Managerial and Organisational Constraints

All managers operate under a series of constraints imposed by the organisation or agency and by the management environment. Managers as individuals must respond to organisational objectives in carrying out their duties. Managers are not only responsible for implementing projects swiftly and competently but also must do so within the context of the organisation's long-range goals and objectives.

The organisation itself operates within a complex legal, social, economic and political environment, and disaster managers find themselves accountable to donors, government administrators, disaster victims, the general public and others as well as to their own organisation. Organisations exist in a society which not only has expectations from them but also places constraints on what objectives they can seek. Thus while organisational objectives influence the manager, the larger environment may dictate these objectives.

Managers themselves have personal characteristics that help determine the way they perform. They have abilities, skills, traits, interests, needs, and aspirations which have been shaped and formed by their experiences. These characteristics influence the manner in which managers interpret and act on demands dictated by the objectives of the organisation. The uniqueness of each managerial personality accounts for much of the variation in the way managerial activities are carried out. At the same time, the more general nature of organisational objectives accounts for the continuity and similarity in managerial activity within each institution or agency.

Managerial activities are also affected by certain characteristics of the immediate work environment such as the nature of subordinates' tasks and the technology available to accomplish those tasks. For example, the managerial activities required to plan, organise, and control routine tasks with simple technology may be different from those required for a non-routine task using complex technology. Other work-related factors include the amount of authority delegated to managers and the qualities of the interpersonal relationships between managers and their subordinates.

In addition to work-related influences, non-work related factors affect managerial activities. Managers belong to various friendship and interest groups whose influence may be reflected in a manager's work. For example, group pressure can cause managers to emphasise technical activities at the expense of human relations activities, or vice versa. (So can background, education and the tools at hand.)

The performance of managers influences the work of their subordinates. The objectives are to stimulate a coordinated effort and achieve a high performance. Yet the manager is only one influencing factor. Subordinates bring to the job their own unique sets of personal characteristics including abilities, interests and traits, and they also belong to groups which exert non-work-related influence. The outcome of these multiple and often conflicting factors is performance which itself becomes an influence on organisational goals and on managers as individuals.

Managerial Environments

The managerial environment for disaster managers is filled with uncertainties.

— *Turbulent Environment*: A turbulent environment changes frequently. After a disaster, changes may occur in political, legal and economic sectors that create confusion. This confusion often results in less-than reliable information reaching decision makers. It is difficult for managers to assess where relief supplies are needed and what the priorities are as the situation changes.

— *Hostile Environment*: A hostile environment is one that contains risk. Relief agencies often operate in areas where there is political instability or restraint. A hostile environment exists if relief is restricted for political reasons.

— *Diverse Environment*: A diverse environment exists if the organisation's various service areas have differing needs. For example, an agency operating in both urban and rural areas will probably have to cope with different victim needs and preferences. The differences may require different delivery models and types of assistance.

A diverse environment also exists when an agency offers services in several different sectors such as housing, health, etc., such relief agencies provide food, shelter, medical services and social services. Each of these requires different technology, materials and information. The legal and political constraints on each of the services are also different.

— *Technically Complex Environment*: A technically complex environment exists if sophisticated information is needed to make important decisions. As a general rule housing, agriculture and public health sectors operate in technically complex environments. Long-range planning, systematic information systems and technical personnel are required in order to operate in these sectors.

Changing Values

It is common today to hear relief experts calling for more "accountability" or "social responsibility" on the part of every type of relief or development organisation. These demands for more social awareness and responsibility from the relief agencies are an attempt to make the institutions more responsive to human needs. Disaster managers will increasingly be called upon to react to these demands.

The increasing demands on relief organisations for improved performance and greater social responsibility to disaster victims are resulting in a serious rethinking of the fundamental values and approaches of these organisations. Some executives have responded: "How can society question us? We are operating for humanitarian reasons under difficult circumstances." The root of the conflict lies in two differing approaches to relief-the traditional or "logistics" approach and the "development" approach.

The traditional approach has one clear-cut purpose: to provide immediate humanitarian aid (usually materials and medical services) as quickly as possible after the onset of the disaster. As noted previously, this approach has been attacked as being short-sighted and often counter-productive.

The competing view is the "development" approach which assumes limitless social responsibility. In this approach, managers accept accountability to many different segments of society, and disaster programmes have comprehensive aims far removed from the strict, limited objectives of the relief programmes. Obviously, the above descriptions represent two opposite extremes. The disaster manager must find a way to meet immediate needs and at the same time lay the groundwork for development-oriented activities. A major task of disaster managers and the agencies that they lead is to find a position which will take into account victims' needs and expectations and at the same time meet the organisation's responsibilities to the donors.

Programme Planning

The delivery of all forms of disaster assistance can be

improved through detailed programme planning and sound programme management. Programme planning is the more important, for if all aspects of the programme are thoroughly considered, if objectives are clearly defined and tasks are properly sequenced, many of the management problems that often develop can be avoided. Programme planning is not difficult and does not take a lot of time. The following is a description of some of the key considerations and steps in programme planning and management.

The planning function includes all managerial activities which determine the programme's objectives and the appropriate means to achieve these objectives. In order to analyse the planning function in more specific terms, the function can be broken down into six interrelated steps:

— *Step 1:* Determining how and where the agency can provide assistance.

— *Step 2:* Stating and implementing policies which direct activities toward the desired objectives.

— *Step 3:* Establishing goals and objectives and putting them in order according to priority.

— *Step 4:* Quantifying objectives.

— *Step 5:* Determining strategies and approaches for implementation.

— *Step 6:* Making the plans operational through budgeting and resource allocation.

Determining How and Where to Intervene

The first step in intervention is deciding how and where the agency can be most helpful. One of the first activities following a disaster is disaster assessment. There are three types of assessment: damage assessment, needs assessment and situation assessment. For most relief and reconstruction programmes, needs assessment is the more critical during the emergency phase of an operation. Needs can best be determined by visiting representative areas and talking to selected groups in the affected communities. Emergency needs are usually obvious; long-term needs may be more difficult to ascertain. Furthermore, needs change from day to day. What is important is identifying the needs at the times they must be met.

Once the basic needs have been identified, they should be quantified. Agencies should be careful not to become too involved in surveying but should attempt to estimate percentages of families requiring different types of assistance.

> "A count needs to be taken of the reserves of food, medicine, clothing and building materials existing within the community, and of the capacity of the victims to help themselves and each other. Rarely will everyone in the area be stricken, and of those who are, not all will take advantage of the relief offered."

The next step is to determine what gaps exist in the overall delivery of assistance. Agencies should remember that usually other relief organisations will provide aid, and their plans should be taken into account before the agency decides which activities it will undertake in any particular area.

Initial Steps in Programme Planning

Once an agency has decided on a certain course of action, the next step is to define precisely what the programme hopes to achieve, and to establish a framework for guiding the decisions that will be required in subsequent activities. To do this, an agency first sets its policies, then establishes goals and objectives, and finally selects the strategies and approaches by which to attain the objectives. The process sounds simple and, in fact, it is. Yet it is surprising how many agencies fail to utilise it and flounder because no one is sure precisely what the goals of the programme are.

Setting Policies

Policies are used to shape the response. They provide a framework or standard by which choices are evaluated. Setting policy is one of the easiest of all the programme planning steps. Unfortunately it is the one that is the most often neglected and is often made more difficult by limited mandates of the organisation or by prior constraints set by donors. Ideally, an agency that frequently responds to disasters sets flexible policies as part of its preparedness activities; when a disaster occurs, those involved in the initial programme have a general guide for structuring their decision making.

Policy-making ensures that action is objective oriented. Policies determine how the objectives are to be achieved (the strategies). Managerial control includes specification of action before the fact, and policies serve this end. Effective policies must be:

1. *Flexible*: A policy must strike a reasonable balance between stability and flexibility. Conditions change and policies must change to meet them. On the other hand, some degree of stability must prevail if order and a sense of direction are to be achieved.
2. *Comprehensive*: A policy must cover any contingency. The degree of comprehensives depends upon the scope of action encompassed by the policy itself. If the policy is directed toward very narrow ranges of activity-for example, hiring policies-it need not be as comprehensive as a policy concerned with broader issues.
3. *Coordinative*: A policy must provide for the coordination of the various sub-units of the

organisation whose actions are interrelated. Without coordinative direction provided by policies, each sub-unit is tempted to pursue its own objectives. The ultimate test of any sub-unit's activity should be its relationship to the policy statement.

4. *Clear*: A policy must be stated clearly and logically. It must specify the intended aim of the action which it governs, define the appropriate methods and action, and establish the limits of freedom of action permitted to decision-makers and subordinates.

Setting Objectives

Managers must consider three aspects of objectives: the priority of each objective; its timing; and its delegation to the appropriate person or department in the organisation.

Priority of Objectives

In programme planning, the accomplishment of certain objectives may be relatively more important than others. Therefore, the establishment of priorities is extremely important so that the resources of the organisation can be allocated rationally. Managers are constantly confronted with alternative objectives which must be evaluated and ranked. Of course, the determination of objectives and priorities is often a judgmental decision and, therefore, can be difficult.

Timing

An organisation's activities are guided by different objectives depending upon the duration of the action and the point in time at which they are being carried out. In emergency operations, it is common to refer to actions as "short-term" (those that take place in the period immediately before, during or after an emergency), "intermediate" (those that take place in the transitional or rehabilitation phase), and "long-term" (those that take place during the reconstruction or recovery period or long before a disaster). The relationship between priority and timing is quite close since the objectives tend to be stated in terms of "ultimates," that is, those objectives which must be accomplished in order to ensure the continuity of a programme in each successive time phase.

Delegating Objectives

Because agencies are organised into department according to function—e.g., procurement, operations, finance—or by area, it is important that objectives be assigned to the appropriate person or department in the agency to be carried out.

The delegation of objectives should be reviewed for conflicts and problems of coordination, because in certain cases achieving the objectives in one department may make it difficult to achieve objectives in another. For example, a procurement objective of lowering procurement costs by mass purchase of low-cost, short-life materials may conflict with an operational objective of providing high-quality, durable materials. This problem can be resolved by a careful review of objectives and the balancing of objectives through group consensus (with the understanding that the objectives of neither unit can be maximised).

Conflicts in Objective Setting

Many diverse groups have interests in the operation of relief agencies that are potentially in conflict. At any point, disaster victims, the agency's staff, donors, suppliers and governmental oversight groups are all concerned with the operation of an agency. During the process of setting objectives, the relative importance of these interest groups must be recognised, and the plans must incorporate and integrate their interests.

Some of the most common planning trade-offs faced by managers in relief organisations are the following:

1. Short-term *versus* long-term programmes.
2. "Relief" *versus* "development" programmes.
3. Service to present areas *versus* expanding to new areas.

Measurement of Objectives

Objectives must be stated in terms that are understandable and measurable to those who must achieve them. In fact, there is evidence which clearly indicates that specific, measurable objectives increase both staff and organisational performance and that difficult objectives, if accepted by employees, result in better performance than easier objectives.

The real difficulty lies in determining what should be measured in each area, and how it should be measured. The more abstract the objective, the more difficult it is to measure performance. An obvious side effect of the necessity for measurable objectives is the tendency in some organisations to focus attention on the measurement and away from the true substance of the objective. A relief agency which measures accomplishment in terms of numbers of persons receiving aid, instead of quality of supplies delivered and the benefit provided, exemplifies over concern for the measurement process instead of what is being measured.

Quantifying Objectives

The fourth step in programme planning is the quantification of objectives. The purpose is to determine how much assistance is to be provided and how many beneficiaries there will be. (It is at this point that the quantification's provided by the different parts of the disaster assessment are helpful.)

Determining Strategies and Approaches

Determination of strategies and approaches is the fifth step in conceptualising a relief or reconstruction programme. A strategy is the plan for attaining a goal, while an approach is the method used. The following example should clarify the differences. To provide replacement housing after a disaster, some strategies open to an agency are:

1. To provide indirect assistance by stimulating the housing industry;
2. To provide direct assistance by giving loans and grants;
3. To provide direct assistance by establishing a construction programme.

Assuming that the strategy chosen by an agency is to establish a housing programme, some approaches that might be available include:

1. To provide the needed construction materials and tools;
2. To provide materials and technical assistance in an "aided" self-help construction programme;
3. To establish a construction team and build the frames and roofs of houses, but leave the remainder of the construction and finishing details to the homeowner;
4. To establish a construction team and build complete replacement houses for a designated number of people in the project area.

The selection of one strategy or approach should not preclude the adoption of others if the resources of the agency allow. It is especially important that approaches be balanced and complementary.

Setting Up the Programme

Once an organisation has defined its programme, the process of putting it into operation begins. This means finding funds, allocating resources, developing programme management, and monitoring the projects.

Budgeting and Resource Allocation

The allocation of resources, especially money, is one of the most difficult choices that an agency will face. It involves a continuing process of estimating financial and other resource needs, obtaining the money and materials, then adjusting the budget based on the resources received. There are some general concepts that are helpful in stretching funds:

1. *Linking to other programmes*: This is the simplest and most effective way to expand the capabilities of an organisation. The methods usually considered are cost-sharing, pooling of resources, or contributing matching funds.
2. *Recoverable funding*: In recoverable funding, all or a portion of the funds distributed are returned to the programme (usually for reinvestment). The most common examples are revolving loans and sales or subsidy schemes. Recoverable funding increases the number of people who can be served and extends the "service" of the cash originally allocated.
3. *Maximisation of buying power*: This refers to the practice of selectively spending money so that the financial power of either the programmes or the

beneficiaries is extended. For example, if loans are determined to be a viable option, an agency can use its money to guarantee loans from usual financial institutions to clients who normally would not be eligible, instead of using its own resources to make the loans.

4. *Multiple objective planning*: In this approach, expenditures are targeted so that more than one objective is realised with each disbursement. This can be accomplished by injecting money into the community in such a way that most of it will stay in the community or at least pass through several hands before leaving.

Methods for Balancing a Programme

The following are methods for balancing a programme:

1. *Concentration of resources*: To have the maximum effect on a community, a programme should concentrate its resources in a specific geographic area. The size of the area should be such that funding activities are complementary and expenditures in one sector can have an effect on other sectors in the same community. For example, if an agency is funding a housing programme in one community and an agricultural recovery programme in another, the result will be less effective than if they were in the same community, and the overall cost will be higher.
2. *Balance between family and community assistance*: Most international relief agencies, especially the Volags, tend to respond to disasters with programmes to assist families. Community assistance is commonly left to the government and its donors. In certain situations, it may seem difficult for an agency to coordinate its activities so that both families and

communities receive assistance concurrently and a degree of balance is attained. Yet full recovery is not complete until all sectors are restored to normal, and the government's resources are often very limited. For this reason, it may be necessary to provide assistance to community projects as well as to families, especially following large disasters in remote rural areas where governmental assistance is likely to come slowly, if at all. As a rule, agencies should allocate one-fourth to one-third of the project funds for labour-intensive community projects in these situations.

3. *Balanced financial assistance*: Before deciding how to provide financial assistance to families, the financial capabilities of the average family to be served should be considered. Rather than provide all assistance free, it may be possible to sell some items at full or greatly reduced prices. Some victims of a disaster can qualify for loans rather than grants. It should be remembered that grants or donations are non-recoverable and an assistance programme will soon be out of business if this course is followed. Therefore, an agency should develop a balanced portfolio of financial assistance prior to initiating operations.

Estimating Needs and Resources

The first step in resource allocation is estimating both needs and resources. The two basic issues that must be resolved are: (1) what types and levels of needs will be encountered during the planning period, and (2) what level of resources will be available to meet the needs. This process is called forecasting and determines the level and timing of financial and material resources required to sustain operations.

Forecasting is the process of using past and current information to predict future events. There are four widely used methods, each of which requires its own type of data. These methods range in degree of sophistication from the hunches of experienced managers to specialised models.

— *Hunches*: Hunches are estimates of future events based upon past experience. The "hunch" approach is relatively cheap and usually effective if the person making the hunch has a thorough knowledge of the project area, practice in programming, and a background of working in similar projects.

— *Surveys*: Surveys are research efforts carried out by staff in the field to provide more data (usually to verify other forecasts). By means of statistical sampling techniques, the forecaster can often compile enough information to identify a range of needs.

— *Time-Series*: Time-series analysis is simply the analysis of the relationship between needs and time.

The advantages and disadvantages to using time-series analysis can be seen by looking at the two basic types of disasters. In cataclysmic or rapid onset disasters such as earthquakes or hurricanes, emergency needs occur quickly, rise rapidly and then fall fairly steadily. For long-term, continuing disasters such as civil wars and droughts, needs may rise sporadically and continuously for long periods of time.

— *Comparative Modelling*: Comparative Modelling permits the forecaster to analyse the relationship between needs and a number of independent variables and to predict needs based on similar patterns of need from past disasters.

One method which can be used for modelling assistance needs following a rapid onset disaster begins with identification of the variables which are normally encountered in a particular type of disaster. Among the obvious variables are locale, season, setting (urban or rural), availability of local resources, and people's preferences. For example, shelter demands will be greater and more immediate in a cold, wet climate than in a dry, mild climate.

Trends regarding needs and demands from previous operations are identified and charted on a time-series graph and compared with the demands and needs of the present operation. By comparing present needs with the curve representing past experience, the manager can forecast future needs. The needs in the current operation are approximately 50 percent greater than the trend from past operations. Thus, a manager could reasonably predict that needs in three weeks would be approximately 50 percent greater than the needs for the same time period from previous disasters.

In order for an organisation to operate, it must have the necessary resources. Accordingly, it is necessary to forecast the future availability of personnel, materials and capital. The techniques of forecasting resources are virtually the same as those employed to forecast operations-that is, hunches, surveys, time-series analysis, and modelling.

Forecasting Needs

Forecasting needs in long-term, slow onset disasters such as droughts or refugee crises is a problem often faced by emergency managers. Situations where refugees are continuing to arrive and the conditions that are displacing them are not predicted to change in the immediate future demand that effective contingency planning, especially for food supplies, receive a high priority. Contingency planning consists of estimating the number of new arrivals and ordering and pre-positioning supplies. Because refugee situations are fluid, it is often difficult to estimate the number of people that may require help. Among the factors that must be considered are:

1. Enough supplies must be ordered to meet the needs of new arrivals without:
   (a) over ordering;
   (b) drawing on supplies for refugees already under care;
   (c) overloading storage and transport capacity (thus resulting in spoilage and increased chance of pilferage).
2. Sufficient lead time must be factored into any purchases that require shipment from abroad, to allow for transit time.
3. Local purchases must be handled in such a way that they do not cause price increases or shortages for local people.

A formula that may be used for estimating the potential number of new arrivals is described below. This formula provides planners with:

— an estimate of how many people may be in need of assistance during a specified, limited period;

— a number that can be used to determine if the supplies they have on hand or in the pipeline could meet the needs of new arrivals;

— a number that will permit an agency to order the necessary supplies without over ordering or overloading the logistics system.

In most droughts and refugee situations, new arrivals appear over a period of time; i.e., after the initial influx, the percentage of new arrivals rarely doubles instantaneously. The new arrivals rarely come in a steady flow; rather they usually come in waves triggered by specific events. Thus, contingency plans must be constantly updated, and agencies should adopt a flexible basis for determining numbers rather than trying to guess the total and stockpiling for that number.

Budgeting

The next step in resource allocation is the development of budgets for each important element of the programme. Money is the oil that keeps the relief machine running smoothly; thus simple, accurate systems that improve budgeting and cost control are crucial. Budgeting for post-disaster programmes is usually a trial-and-error process, especially for Volags. Because Volags usually raise their relief money through appeals to the public or by submitting proposals to government or inter-governmental organisations, they rarely know precisely how much money they will have for the operation when they start out. This, coupled with the uncertainties that exist until the disaster assessment is completed, makes it difficult to prepare a budget.

The popular preconception is that budgets are overestimated in the early stages when financial resources are plentiful or that an agency expands its activities beyond the resources available. In practice, this is usually not the case. Some disasters attract an outpouring of aid, and if the major donor governments become involved, substantial resources will be available. More often, the problem is trying to allocate resources wisely or to establish programmes that match the capabilities of an organisation, rather than not having sufficient resources.

Many agencies tend to develop fixed, inflexible budgets early in a programme. In agencies where rigid financial policies exist, a quickly prepared budget may inadvertently become an instrument that controls the programme, rather than vice versa.

The most realistic way to overcome budgeting problems is for an agency to establish a policy on how and when it will commit its funds in each phase of the disaster. For example, some agencies place a significant portion (up to 75 percent) of all funds received from initial appeals into a contingency fund for use in longer-term programmes during reconstruction. This allows the field staff to develop more realistic budgets in the later stages of recovery.

Whatever approach is used, a budget must be flexible and especially anticipate inflation of costs in the disaster area. If it is formulated during the initial stages of a disaster, a large portion of the total budget should be left in uncommitted contingency reserve so that the field staff can adapt to the changing situation and respond to unmet needs.

Many agencies experience difficulty with monetary control and have trouble accounting for funds. Usually this is because they do not use accounting systems that are adapted to a disaster situation. Good field accounting requires a simple system that is easy to use, easy to carry, and places the emphasis of trust on the user; and it requires training in how to use the system before disaster strikes. Field representatives, especially in the emergency, must have an accounting system that recognises the need for flexibility and simplicity. Several agencies have recently begun to use simplified field-account books that have built-in impression pads, so that duplicate or triplicate records can be prepared and maintained. This innovation reflects the agencies' awareness that a disaster creates special accounting needs.

There is a close relationship between budgeting as a planning technique and budgeting as a control technique.

In this section we are concerned only with the preparation of budgets prior to operations.

From this perspective, budgeting is a part of planning. However, with the passage of time and as the organisation engages in its activities, the actual results are compared with the budgeted (planned) results. This analysis may lead to corrective action. Thus, budgeting can be viewed as a method for evaluating and coordinating the efforts of the organisation.

Budgeting Approaches

The value of budgets as a planning tool depends on how flexible they are to changing conditions. The forecasted data are based upon certain assumptions about the future. If these assumptions prove wrong, the budgets are inadequate. (Unfortunately, contracting procedures of many major donor organisations do not take disaster conditions into consideration and continue to rely on fixed budgets.)

In disasters, a fixed budget is difficult to use because situations, especially in an emergency, change rapidly. Thus a more flexible type of budget is needed. This is particularly important in refugee emergency operations when neither the total number of refugees nor the length of the operation is known. Two ways to provide flexibility in budgeting are variable budgeting and moving budgeting.

Variable Budgeting

Variable budgeting provides for the possibility that actual costs deviate from planned costs. It recognises that certain costs are variable while others are fixed. In this case, the cost of the land needed to situate the refugees is fixed, i.e., it is the same no matter how many people are placed on the site. The cost of shelters, however, is variable. The initial costs (for equipment, tools, etc.) are higher on a per-shelter basis but can be pro-rated for later shelters, thereby reducing the per-unit shelter cost.

Moving Budgeting

Moving budgeting is the preparation of a budget for a fixed period, say, one year, with periodic updating at fixed intervals, say, one month. For example, a budget is prepared in December for the next year, January through December. At the end of January, the budget is revised and projected for the next 12 months, February through January. In this manner, the most recent information is included in the budgeting process. Premises and assumptions are constantly revised as management monitors the programme.

Moving budgets have the advantage of systematic re-examination, but have the disadvantage of being time consuming to maintain.

Common Problems in Programme Planning

An analysis of programme planning in a number of recent relief operations reveals common errors.

1. *Poor definition of the project*: Not enough can be said about this topic. The vast majority of relief and reconstruction programmes are conducted without the establishment of formal goals or objectives. Often there are vague statements such as "to help the victim" or "to reconstruct houses." Until the staff has defined where a project is going, it will be difficult to determine how to get there.

2. *Failure to establish policies to shape programme planning*: Policies provide the framework within which the staff makes choices throughout the programme planning process. Failure to establish policies early leaves a programme without any

guiding principles and with no firm basis upon which to make decisions.

3. Failure to involve the local people fully in the planning process.
4. *Failure to examine the complete range of options*: Too often, an agency selects the first approach to solving a particular problem that is proposed. Usually this is a matter of not taking enough time to explore the choices or not being familiar with the possible alternatives.
5. *Selection of only one strategy or approach to problem-solving*: Often an organisation will "fixate" on a particular methodology and will develop a whole programme around one standard approach. If anything goes wrong or if the approach meets with only limited success, the entire programme may have to be restructured. Furthermore, the selection of only one approach does not easily accommodate variances within the affected area.
6. *Failure to balance the programme*: A balanced programme meets a variety of related needs. For example, a housing reconstruction programme that provides training in improved construction techniques, job opportunities for local builders and craftsmen, employment opportunities so that local people can gain the funds necessary to participate in the programme, and supplementary projects designed to improve the sites and services (such as sanitation) would be considered a balanced programme. A programme that simply provides a replacement for a damaged house would not.
7. *Over-extension*: Programmes become over-extended by: (1) trying to meet too many needs, (2) trying to meet the needs of too many people, or (3) trying to meet the needs in too broad an area. A good

example of over-extension occurred in Guatemala after the 1976 earthquake when a small relief agency with a very small staff offered to provide housing reconstruction services to a geographic area of more than 1500 square kilometres that had not only a rural population, but also a number of large towns. The total number of people in the area approached 75,000. When the programme made a commitment to the government to provide services in this area, it had only received a total of $25,000 for reconstruction. During the course of the agency's efforts, it received an additional $25,000 and some roofing material as an in-kind contribution from a foreign government, bringing the total monetary resources of the agency to approximately $80,000. Had the agency been able to use the entire amount, the number of people effectively served could not have been more than approximately 10 percent of those in the project area.

8. *Failure to examine cause-and-effect relationships:* Failure to look ahead is often a result of inexperience. Yet by thinking through many of the programme options and trying to estimate the outcome, agencies could avoid many mistakes. As a part of the planning process, agencies should consider preparing a programme impact assessment similar to the environmental impact statements that are required of many construction projects.
9. *Failure to budget properly*: Estimating budgets for disaster operations is difficult. Not only must a budget be prepared in an inflationary environment, but the amount of funds and their date of transfer to the programme are often unknown.

10. *Failure to obtain proper technical inputs*: This is often a result of failure by the agencies to expand their horizons and an attempt to oversimplify their humanitarian work. In most cases, agencies are usually not aware of all the related issues or of the technical expertise that is available.

    Another aspect of this problem is the use of inappropriate technical inputs. For example, following many disasters, agencies send medical teams with the latest technical equipment and medicines. In most cases, however, what is needed is not high-tech curative medicine but low-technology, community-based preventive health measures, such as sanitation and hygiene.

    The use of technology and selection of the appropriate technology is always a problem for agencies with no prior experience in the affected community and with scant knowledge of the society.

11. Lack of coordination with other relief agencies and government programmes: Agencies often fail to consider the activities being planned or conducted in their project area by other organisations. This oversight may occur through simple lack of contact and/or communication or through a political refusal to recognise the efforts of any other organisation. In either case, the end result is inappropriate programme planning, which in turn, often leads to duplication of effort, projects which work at cross-purposes, and a general waste of resources. A far more effective approach is to establish a good working relationship with other agencies and, if possible, establish a planning council to minimise these problems. At the very least, project managers should keep well-informed of the activities of other

agencies operating within the same region as their programmes.

DECISION-MAKING

All managers must sooner or later make decisions. That is, they face several alternatives, and their decision involves a comparison between the alternatives and an evaluation of the outcome. The quality of the decisions managers make is the true measure of their performance. Each operational decision influences future actions, which in turn, require further decisions. Errors in decision making, therefore, tend to be cumulative.

Decision-making is the major responsibility of a disaster manager, regardless of his or her functional area or level in the organisation. Some of these decisions may have a strong impact on the organisation, while others will be important but less crucial. The important point, however, is that all will have some sort of effect.

Variables in Decision-Making

In some cases, decisions are made where there are few alternatives and all the parameters of the decision can be clearly identified. Many decisions, however, require that a choice be made between different courses which may be affected by variables or events beyond a manager's control. For example, the field director of a refugee relief operation knows that the accuracy of new arrival forecasts will depend in large measure upon political events in another country. Similarly, a supply officer of a relief agency is faced with the problem of how much and what types of supplies should be ordered in the immediate aftermath of an earthquake, without knowing the full extent of the disaster.

Decision making is carried out under three different conditions or sets of variables: certainty, risk, and uncertainty.

Certainty

When a manager knows or is certain of all the effects of variables on an issue, "certainty" exists. This means that the manager should be able to make accurate decisions when these circumstances exist. Of course, this type of decision-making environment is rare.

Suppose the manager of a relief agency has been alerted by an early warning system that 2000 refugees will arrive in his refugee camp in one week. He would be foolish not to order supplies for 2000 people and prepare to distribute them.

The decision-maker in this example is fortunate because accurate information about future events is available. In most situations, the manager does not know exactly what will occur. Under these conditions, the manager is forced to use probabilities to make decisions.

Risk

In some situations, a manager is able to estimate the probability that certain variables could occur. The ability to estimate may be due to experience, incomplete but reliable information or, in some cases, an accurate report. When estimates are made, a degree of risk is involved, but some amount of information about the situation is available. The situation requires estimating the probability that one or more known variables might influence the decision being made. If the basis for the decision is stated in terms of maximising results—e.g., service levels—the decision maker would select the alternative which produces the best result. However, if the basis for the decision is stated in terms of minimising the outcome—e.g., costs—the decision maker would select the alternative which minimises the results.

Uncertainty

A condition of uncertainty exists when a manager is faced with reaching a decision with no historical data concerning the variables and/or unknowns and their probability of occurrence. In these circumstances, the manager can decide:

— to maximise the possible results;
— to minimise the results;
— to maximise the results that are the minimum possible under the circumstances;
— to minimise the maximum possible results;
— to avoid or delay the decision.

Types of Decisions

There are three types of decisions in disaster management:

1. *Routine (or programmed) decisions*: If a problem or situation occurs often, a routine procedure is usually developed for solving it. Thus decisions are programmed to the extent that they are routine and repetitive and a specific procedure has been developed for handling them. Examples would be purchasing relief supplies, handling personnel matters, and dealing with problems that were anticipated. Routine decisions are normally guided by policies, guidelines or procedures.
2. *Non-routine (or non-programmed) decisions*: When problems are broad, novel and unanticipated, they require decisions that have not been covered in the organisation's planning (i.e., they have not been programmed). As such, there is no established procedure for handling the problem.

3. *Technically-guided decisions*: In many cases, determination of which course to choose is guided by technical factors beyond the control of the manager. For example, flood victims often demand that relief agencies provide "flood-proof" houses. Unfortunately, flooding is a site problem, not a structural one. Therefore, a decision not to provide housing assistance on the same site would be guided by technical, not humanitarian, considerations.

Process of Decision-Making

The starting point in any analysis of decision-making involves a determination of whether a decision needs to be made. The first step is to identify the problem and the kinds of decisions required to solve this problem. However, before making a decision, the manager develops a number of possible alternatives (or potential solutions to the problem) and considers the potential results and possible consequences of each.

Up to this point, the process is fairly simple; it is choosing the best alternative that becomes complicated. In business, there are various decision models to help managers select the best course with the least risk. However, for the disaster manager, the tools are limited. The setting of policies, goals and objectives can help narrow the choices and provide a framework for decision-making. When a decision needs to be made, the manager reviews each alternative that he/she has selected to determine if it is consistent with the organisational objectives and overall policy and if it will further the operational goals and objective of the programme and/or organisation.

If a policy is established or a specific rule or procedure is developed to guide decisions, it will not be necessary to develop and evaluate alternatives each time a problem arises. (However, over time, the policies may have to be reviewed and updated.)

Most decisions that managers must make can be structured, and repetitive problems in their daily operations can be handled with policies and procedures or according to technical feasibility. These decisions should be treated as routine without expending unnecessary resources or time on them. It is non-programmed decisions that are the concern of the disaster manager, since this is the type of decision most likely to be encountered in an emergency. These deal with unknowns and, therefore, can have a potentially greater negative impact if handled improperly.

Non-Programmed: Non-programmed decisions have traditionally been handled by general problem solving processes, judgement, intuition and creativity. In pyramidal organisations, during non-crisis situations, non-programmed decisions are usually the concern of top management, while middle-level and field-level managers generally make programmed decisions. The result is that decision making is cumbersome, time consuming, and not as effective or timely. In organisations where authority is shared or resides at the field level, both programmed and non-programmed decisions are made at all levels.

Disasters, however, demand that non-routine decisions be made at all levels, and field-level managers, especially in emergencies, most often deal with non-programmed decisions. Thus, to improve the performance of relief operations, it is necessary to improve the non-programmed decision-making capabilities of field-level managers.

Two ways to improve decision-making under these circumstances are:

1. To structure the decision-making process;
2. To provide a policy framework against which to measure choices.

Steps in Decision-Making

In order to make decisions under non-routine, emergency circumstances, the following steps should be taken:

1. *Define the problem and the decision to be made*: Clarify the problem and try to eliminate irrelevant or unnecessary issues.
2. *Gather and collate all the information about the problem*: Put all the information in a logical form and sequence.
3. Extract the relevant information.
4. *Evaluate the information*: Assess the quality and accuracy of the information and estimate the unknowns and variables that may influence the outcome of the decision.
5. *Identity alternatives*: Determine the alternatives and the possible outcomes of each.
6. Make the decision.

Once a decision has been made, it should be adhered to. Hesitation or wavering breeds uncertainty and lack of confidence in the decision maker and can reduce the effectiveness of the decision.

INFORMATION MANAGEMENT

Effective planning requires information. The quality of a decision depends greatly on an accurate understanding of the circumstances surrounding an issue and on knowledge of the available alternatives. The better the information, the better the resulting decision. The development of an information system helps to manage both existing and incoming information.

Information management can be likened to the four-stroke cycle of a conventional internal combustion engine:

1. Information in (acquisition) (Intake)
2. Assessment or evaluation (Compression)
3. Decision making (Ignition)
4. Information out (decision implementation Exhaust)

The task of generating data for managerial decision making should be viewed as the function of an information management system. This "...is a scheme according to which...information is provided, in the right amount, to the right persons, at the right time. Determining what information to include and how to package this information depends on the person to whom the information is to be addressed and the reason for which it is given. Thus, an information system carefully distinguishes, for example, between...reports from the project manager to top management, and daily progress reports the manager receives from the project staff." It supports the planning, control, and operations functions of an organisation by providing information for use in decision-making.

Information requirements vary depending on the level in the organisation and the type of decision being made. In every case, it is vital that appropriate information be directed to the proper decision maker. In this context, every organisation can be viewed as an information/decision system.

Classes of Information

The types as well as sources of information will vary, but generally there are three classes of information:

— *Planning Information*: This type of information relates to the tasks of formulating objectives, determining the amounts and kinds of resources necessary to attain the objectives, and the policies that govern their use. Much of this information will come from external sources and will relate to such factors as the present and predicted situation in the operational area, availability of resources (material, financial and human), and the political environment. This information forms the input to the non-programmed types of decisions made at each level in the organisation.

— *Control Information*: This information aids managers to make decisions which are consistent with the achievement of organisational objectives and to see how efficiently resources are being used. It enables managers to determine if "actual results" are meeting "planned-for results" (objectives). It relies heavily on internal sources of information and involves such problems as developing budgets and measuring the performance of personnel. The nature of problems faced at this level may result in either programmed or non-programmed types of decisions.

— *Operational Information*: This information relates to the day-to-day activities of the organisation. Operational data is usually required in regard to three broad categories: people, property, and the operation (or status) of emergency services. It includes routine and necessary types of information such as financial accounting, inventory control, and scheduling. Most of the information is generated internally, and since it usually relates to specific tasks, it often comes from designated subordinates. Field-level managers are the primary users of this information.

Information Flows

There are two types of information flow in a management information system. An external information flow is information that either comes to or is sent from the organisation. An intra-organisational flow is information flowing within the organisation.

External information includes the inward flow of information, called intelligence, and the outward flow, called organisational communications.

Intelligence information includes data on the various elements of the organisation's operating environment such as victims, other agencies, relief suppliers, and the local government. It also includes information on trends and patterns, as well as developments in the social and cultural environment in which the organisation operates. This type of information has long-term significance to the organisation and aids in long-range, strategic planning.

The disaster manager receives four distinct types of disaster intelligence:

1. *Early-Warning Reports*: E-W reports provide data about pending events. Most E-W reports are issued prior to cyclones, floods and droughts and are used to provide preparedness information and to issue alerts and evacuation information. E-W reports also provide agencies with information concerning expected arrivals of refugees from a war zone and provide data about the numbers of refugees and their condition.

2. *Situation Reports*: S-R are periodic reports prepared by major relief operations. They describe the impact of the emergency as it occurs and provide a rough summary of events. After the disaster, they detail the response by different relief agencies.

3. *Disaster Assessment Reports*: DARs are assessments of a post-disaster situation. They should provide a rough quantification of needs and damages as well as a picture of the magnitude of the overall situation. The assessment should also identify the geographic locations that should receive priority.
4. *Epidemiologic Surveillance*: The health and nutritional status of disaster victims or refugees is provided by data collected as part of epidemiologic surveillance. By monitoring data and trends, the manager can determine current needs and forecast future needs.

Organisational communications flow outward from the organisation to the external operating environment. In the case of a relief agency, any public awareness or other promotional efforts are considered organisational communications and are controlled by the organisation. Although outward information is important, we will not cover the topic in this course.

Information must flow through as well as to and from the organisation. Within every organisation, there are vertical (both upward and downward) and horizontal information flows. The rationale of an information management system is that all information should move according to a formal scheme and direction.

In order to accomplish this, there are three major requirements:

1. *Determining information needs*: Information needs are identified by determining how much information is needed; how, when, and by whom it will be used; and in what form it is needed. The process begins with an examination of the output requirements. One way is to classify information based on the level in the organisation where it will be used. Thus, output requirements would be based on determining what information is necessary for

planning and controlling operations at different organisational levels, what information is needed to allocate resources, and what information is needed to evaluate performance. These types of questions recognize the fact that different kinds of information are needed for formulating organisational objectives than for scheduling operations.

2. *It should be remembered that too much information may actually hinder a manager's performance*: It is important to distinguish "need to know" types of information from "nice to know" information. More information does not necessarily mean better performance.
3. *Information-gathering and processing*: The purpose of this step is to improve the overall quality of the information. It includes six component services:
   - *Collection*: Collection involves gathering and recording information. (It is especially important to write down verbal communications.)
   - *Evaluation*: Evaluation involves determining how much confidence can be placed in a particular piece of information. Such factors as the credibility of the source and the relevance, reliability and validity of the data must be determined.
   - *Abstracting*: Abstracting involves editing and reducing incoming information and data in order to provide the managers with only that information which is relevant to their particular task.
   - *Indexing*: Indexing provides classification for storage and retrieval purposes.

Storage: Storage consists of filing information so that it can be referred to, as needed. It may be needed to defend a decision. Remember: information that is not "captured" is lost forever.

— *Dissemination*: Dissemination entails getting the right information to the right manager at the right time. This is the overriding purpose of an information management system.

4. *Information use.* How information is used depends greatly on its quality (accuracy), how it is presented (form), and its timeliness. These relate to the basic needs determined in the beginning. If the right questions are asked and the system is planned carefully, the user will be provided with relevant information. The goal is to provide the right information to the right decision maker at the right time. In some cases, timeliness may take precedence over accuracy. If information is not available when it is needed, then its accuracy loses importance. In most cases, however, both are critical, and timeliness is determined by the nature of the decisions that must be made. For example, a manager in an earthquake relief operation may find accurate reports of the total number of victims to be only moderately useful, while an official working with civil war refugees needs accurate census information every day.

Establishing a Focal Point for Information Management

It is important that a central focal point be established for the management of information in order to facilitate the flow of information both to and within the organisation. In a large organisation, the focal point may be an office; in a field operation, the focal point is usually an information officer or a person who is assigned information management responsibilities.

Information management in field operations can be significantly improved if facts and information are displayed visually. Displays can be made of tasks, resources available/committed, personnel status and location, and other routine information that is needed continually. Making displays like this should be done as a team-building exercise. This will increase the commitment of all parties concerned to goals, to making the "plan" work; it also increases the practicability of any plan of action by allowing input from the field staff. Displays can be made on chalkboards, graphs, plastic-covered wall boards, or other simple devices. Indeed, simplicity is desirable so that people will be encouraged to keep the information updated. Information-at-a-glance is one of the greatest assets for a disaster manager and for his/her team.

Requirements for Emergency Information Management

Effective information management in emergencies requires the following:

1. The capability of carrying out damage surveys, needs assessment, and reporting (or a reliable source);
2. Facilities to receive, display, collate and assess information;
3. A systematic decision-making process into which the information is fed. (Major decisions are seldom made by the disaster manager alone; more often they are made by a small group or committee in consultation with appropriate specialists. Thus, some system of routing information and assigning it appropriate priority must be established.)

4. Feedback on the reliability/quality/usefulness of the information.

PROGRAMME SUPERVISION, MONITORING AND CONTROL

After a project has begun to function in its assigned areas, regulatory and supervisory measures assume prominence in the project cycle. The term "control" refers to those steps taken to ensure that plans are properly executed. Thus, an important role for a disaster manager is project monitoring and control. This role includes all activities undertaken to ensure that actual operations conform to planned operations.

— Control has been classically defined as 'verifying whether everything occurs in conformity with the plans adopted, the instructions issued, and the principles established'. It therefore follows that, first of all, the plans, instructions, and principles must be clearly defined and understood by everyone, forming the standards or criteria by which performance can unequivocally be measured; lack of initial benchmarks makes control virtually impossible. The purpose of control, then is to find deviations, correct them as early as possible, and prevent them in the future. The nature of project supervision and control thus requires a constant flow of information so that deviations from plans may be spotted and decisions and corrective actions may be taken on time.

— It is important to remember, however, that a deviation between performance and plans is not always the fault of project; a lack of conformity to plans can result from inappropriate plans rather than inadequate performance. Whether the villain is the plan or the non conforming subordinate is sometimes difficult to determine. Planning decisions frequently have to be revised due to errors in judgment and forecasts. Subordinates are sometimes penalised for the superior's planning failures rather than their own performance failures.

— Managers should also recognise that a comparison of plans with performance information may not adequately measure efficiency. The words or data used in the comparison between plans and actual performance must be capable of exact comparison. A great deal of knowledge about environmental, technological, and socio- psychological factors cannot, however, be defined or measured in precise terms.

Control, Coordination and Supervision

Before embarking on a detailed description of the control process and the common pitfalls encountered its course in, let us clarify some of the terms used in this area. "Control" as used herein refers to the use of both active and passive means of ensuring that a project moves along in the general manner in which it was planned. Because emergencies do not afford the manager with the best circumstances under which to obtain planning information, it would be foolish not to assume that some degree of flexibility is permitted in the control process. After all, the objective is not to ensure that the project is run according to plan, but to ensure that it helps the disaster victim or refugee to the greatest extent possible. For this reason, control in disaster management is primarily a function of direct, onsite supervision, coordination and administration.

"Much of the process is informal and indirect and becomes an aspect of the socio-psychological dynamics of the superior-subordinate relationship. Superiors, however, cannot constantly keep watch over their flocks if they are not to be overwhelmed with work. There are also good motivational reasons for not carrying supervision to an extreme. Accounting and other indirect control devices make possible a greater degree of decentralisation and tend to give more personal freedom to subordinates. Therefore, the control process generally involves some combination of onsite supervision and indirect techniques."

Necessary Conditions for Control and Supervision

Three basic conditions are necessary for control:

1. Standards must be established;
2. Information indicating deviations between actual and standard results must be available;
3. Authority to correct problems must be possible.

The logic is clear: without standards, there can be no basis for evaluating the effectiveness of actual performance; without information there can be no way of knowing the situation; without a means to correct problems, the entire control process becomes pointless. The consequences of failure to control are time delays, waste, poor use of resources and, in emergency programmes, increased suffering of the victims and even higher death rates.

Standards are derived from, and have many of the characteristics of, objectives. Standards are targets. To be effective, they must be clearly stated and logically related to the objectives of both the organisation and its programmes. Standards are the criteria against which future, current, or past actions are compared. They are measured in a variety of ways, including physical, monetary, quantitative, and qualitative terms.

In order to implement this measurement process, information must first be obtained which reports actual performance and allows evaluation of performance against standards. Information is most easily acquired for activities which produce specific and concrete results; for example, field-level activities have end products which are easily identified and about which information is readily obtainable. The performance of mid-level departments is more difficult to appraise because the outcome of the activities is difficult to measure.

When a discrepancy occurs between standards and actual performance, the authority to correct problems or to take corrective measures must be assigned to a specific person. The person responsible for taking the corrective steps must know that he/she is responsible and has the authority to take remedial measures. Unless this responsibility is clearly delegated, remedial measures will not be possible.

Finally, channels of communication must be open to people, including staff and victims, at all levels through which information about progress can be conveyed. In order for a programme to be able to adapt and meet needs as they arise, yet still move according to the general plan, it is important to ensure that communication channels are open and that a two-way flow of up-to date information constantly moves through the system.

Types of Control

The control function is broken down into three types according to the stages at which they are applied.

— *Preliminary Control*: Preliminary control is exercised by planning and the assignment of resources to be used in the operation. Human resources must meet the job requirements; materials must meet acceptable levels of quality and must be available at the proper time and place. Equipment must be on hand when needed, and financial resources must be available in the right amounts and at the right times.

— *Monitoring*: Monitoring (or concurrent control) examines actual ongoing operations to ensure that objectives are being met. The principal means by which concurrent control is implemented is through the directing or supervisory activities of managers. Through personal, on-the-spot observation, managers determine whether the work of others is proceeding in the manner defined by policies and procedures. The delegation of authority provides managers with the power to use financial and non- financial incentives to achieve concurrent control. The standards guiding ongoing activity are derived from job descriptions and from policies established by the planning function.

— *Evaluation*: Evaluation (or feedback control) focuses on end results. The corrective action is directed either at improving the process of resource acquisition or modifying future operations. This type of control examines historical results to guide future actions. The methods employed in disaster management include cost-benefit analysis, audit, quality control, performance evaluation, and impact assessment.

The distinction between preliminary control, monitoring, and evaluation enables us to classify certain of the more widely used control techniques as shown in Table 4.1.

Methods for Control

1. *Policies*: Policies are important means for implementing preliminary control, since policies are guidelines for future action. Yet we want to

distinguish between setting policies and implementing them. Setting policy is included in the planning function, whereas implementing policy is a part of the control function.

2. *Job descriptions*: Job descriptions are a part of the control function since they predetermine the activities, responsibilities, and authority of the job holder.

Table 4.1: Control Types and Techniques

Types of Control	*Control Techniques*
Preliminary control	Planning
	Policies
	Standards
	Staffing
	Budgeting
	Material Allotment
Monitoring	Supervision
	Coordination
	Administrative Reporting
Evaluation	Impact Assessment
	Cost-benefit analysis
	Standard cost analysis
	Quality Control procedures
	Employee performance evaluation

3. *Quality control of materials*: The materials to be used in the project must conform to standards of quality. A simple procedure for monitoring quality can be easily explained. Suppose, for example, that management decides it will accept a maximum level of five percent of defective items from a supplier. The material is then inspected by selecting a random sample and calculating the percentage of defective items in that sample. A

decision must then be made, based on the sample, of whether to accept or reject the entire order or to take another sample.

Preliminary control systems for materials should be established as a routine because the decision to accept or reject materials recurs frequently. The standard should be easily measurable and the sample should be easy to take. The decision to accept or reject (or take another sample) can be based upon simple instructions. Thus, the decision becomes automatic. An inspector's instructions may read: "If sample defectives are equal to or more than five percent, take another sample. If sample defectives in second lot exceed five percent, reject lot."

4. *Budgets*: The principal means of controlling the availability and cost (interest) of financial resources is budgeting.

   Budgets should anticipate the ebb and flow of activity during the operating cycle to time the availability of cash to meet obligations. There are two problems in budgeting for relief operations. First, many managers will not have had prior experience with the particular needs of the operation and may not be aware of all the budgeting requirements. A standard budget items list can serve as a checklist for the manager and make sure that all necessary items are considered. (Some organisations include recommended ratios or percentages of the total allocation for each item as a guide for managers. For example, total staff costs of a project may be restricted to a maximum of 20 percent of the total budget.)

   The second problem is keeping enough cash on hand. To aid in the process, some organisations set certain cash-to-commitment ratios. For example, a minimum ratio could be set at 2:1 and the maximum at 3:1 (these ratios recognise the cost of both too little and too much cash on hand.) Corrective action would be taken when the actual current ratio deviates above or below the allowable ratios.

5. *Audit*: Audits are a principal source of information from which managers can evaluate a programme. A management audit is a study of the manner in which the project is being carried out. It focuses primarily on efficiency and management considerations. A financial audit examines the fiscal aspects of the project.
6. *Standard Cost Analysis*: A standard cost system provides information that enables a manager to compare actual costs with pre-determined (standard) costs. The manager must determine the reasons for the variances and decide what corrective action is appropriate. Standard costing may be applied to general or administrative expenses.
7. *Employee Performance Evaluation*: The most important and difficult feedback control technique is employee performance evaluation. It is important because the most crucial resource in any organisation is its people. Evaluation is difficult because the standards for performance are seldom objective or easily identified since managerial and nonmanagerial jobs do not produce things that can be counted, weighed and evaluated in objective terms.
8. *Impact Assessment*: The most important evaluation of a project is the impact assessment. Its purpose is to determine whether the project and its various

activities accomplished the broad as well as specific goals set out during the planning process. The criteria for success in disaster assistance are often very difficult to establish.

5

Understanding Disaster Risk Reduction

During the last fifty years several powerful natural disasters occurred in different parts of the world, in countries large and small, industrialised or agrarian, technologically sophisticated or traditionally focused. The types of natural hazards that triggered these disasters varied from the seemingly unexpected occurrence of earthquakes, to more predictable seasonal floods and periodic storms.

Other less immediate and slowly evolving hazards such as drought and environmental degradation affected even more people with potentially greater costs for their future. More than anything else, the media images of natural disasters at the close of the twentieth century underscored the human consequences and social dimensions of these events.

One need only recall the power of hurricane Mitch that damaged up to 70 percent of the infrastructure in Honduras and Nicaragua in 1998, devastating the economies of all of the Central American countries that are yet to recover fully. This was followed one year later by the worst cyclone in 100 years to hit the Indian state of Orissa, which affected ten times as many people as

Mitch, destroying 18,000 villages in one night. The powerful typhoon Lingling caused extensive damage and over 500 fatalities in the Philippines and Viet Nam at the end of 2001.

Floods of a previously un-remembered scale occurred several times in the past 10 years; in China, Bangladesh and Southern Africa, where people had no recourse but to escape to safety in trees. In 1999, Mexico experienced its worst floods since 1600. Almost 300,000 people were made homeless.

The trend during the last three decades shows an increase in the number of natural hazard events and of affected populations. Even though the number of disasters has more than tripled since the 1970s, the reported death toll has decreased to less than half. Despite losses of US$ 30 billion in 2000, an amount that must, unfortunately, be termed moderate in comparison to the average annual losses during the past decade, both the number of major natural disasters and their costs have increased rapidly in recent years.

In 2000, the insurance industry recorded 850 major loss events in the world, one hundred more than the previous record year in 1999. While the losses recorded in 2000 were lower than the US$ 100 billion incurred in 1999, they provide little comfort to the overall trend during the past decade. Overall the 84 great natural disasters recorded in the 1990s were three times as many as those that occurred the 1960s, whereas the combined economic losses of US$ 591 billion were eight times greater than those of the 1960s.

Ten thousand people died in natural disasters in 2000, compared to more than 70,000 in the previous year, or over 500,000 in the previous ten years. These figures must be treated with caution, as the social and economic cost of disasters is difficult to estimate. By and large, insurance claims tend to be misleading as an estimate of the economic impact of disasters. Considering insured damage claims for the 1999 floods in Austria, Germany and Switzerland, at least 42.5 per cent of damage was covered by disaster insurance. But in Venezuela the same year, only four per cent of flood dam- age was covered.

Generally, disaster statistics tend to be more precise on a smaller scale; in particular on the national and regional level where the evaluation of damages is undertaken in a more systematic manner, based on agreed methodologies. However, this is not the case in all regions and notably in Africa, where the lack of coherent disaster-related figures means the impact of disasters is highly underestimated. In addition, mega-disasters receive much media attention and the setbacks that these events create in the development process are well noted, while some experts estimate that if the pernicious economic impact of the smaller, but recurrent, disasters were assessed, all of these figures would be much higher.

Not appropriately reflected in these statistics are the millions of poor people who have seen their lives indirectly shattered by the economic impact of the natural disasters, their ability to raise a modest income reduced or annihilated and the prospect to escape poverty postponed indefinitely. These losses, modest in absolute economic terms, are devastating at a social and sometimes political level.

There is a demand for reliable and systematic data on disasters by the development sector to assess their socio-economic impact in the short term and, even more importantly, in the long term, if the consequences of the many smaller and unrecorded disasters could be taken into account. While attempted in limited areas, a pressing need remains to consistently document these incremental and often recurrent losses that are continuously eroding the capacities of communities to grow and develop.

While hazards may induce a crisis, it is now widely understood that prevailing conditions within any group of people in a society can determine the extent of their susceptibility or resilience to loss or damage. There is insight across a growing number of professional fields and in some governments that different population segments can be exposed to greater relative risks because of their socio-economic conditions of vulnerability. Because of this, disaster reduction has become increasingly associated with practices that define efforts to achieve sustainable development.

Equally, as the possibility of human-induced influences on climate change are better understood, the detrimental effects of forestry exploitation become evident, or the effectiveness of earlier engineering solutions for controlling natural phenomena are questioned, the relationships between human actions, environmental stewardship and disaster risks are becoming ever more crucial.

It is remarkable that disasters not only affect the poor and traditionally vulnerable countries but also those thought well protected: Canada, the Czech Republic, France, Germany, Poland, the United Kingdom and the United States experienced record-setting floods in recent years of such magnitude that previously accepted procedures for protection and thinking about the utility of structural barriers have to be re-evaluated.

The extraordinarily heavy rainfall associated with hurricane Mitch caused a landslide at the Casita volcano in Nicaragua that was 18 km long and 3 km wide, and totally destroyed three towns and killed more than 2,000 people. Torrential rains triggered the landslide of denuded and unstable slopes in Venezuela in 1999 with more than 20,000 fatalities.

Less than two years later, one of the earthquakes in El Salvador caused a landslide on a slope destabilized by deforestation and slope mining, burying almost 500 people living in ill-placed communities that were probably compromised at least in part by lax control of building regulations.

In 2001 similarly disastrous floods and mudslides caused more than 800 fatalities, most extraordinarily in the Algerian capital, Algiers. The most severe winter storms in a century swept through Canada in 1998, through Western European countries in 1999, and the following year in Mongolia, with even greater loss of livelihoods and longer-term consequences because of the decimated flocks of nomadic herders.

In the past three years, severe earthquakes in Colombia, Greece, India, Peru, Taiwan and Turkey have shaken previously complacent official views on building practices. El Salvador experienced two major earthquakes within one month, one of them measuring 7.6 on the Richter scale, the second strongest in 90 years.

Meanwhile during 2001, persistent drought conditions eroded already fragile livelihoods in Afghanistan and in several other countries of Central Asia, in Eastern and Southern Africa, and in much of Central America. The consequences of uncontrolled wildfire and related conditions of severe atmospheric pollution and haze intruded into neighbouring areas of North-Eastern Africa, Central and North America, South-East Asia, Southern Europe, and within individual states of Australia.

The El Niño/La Niña events of 1997-1998 were the most intense occurrence of this cyclical climatic phenomenon during the twentieth century. Beyond representing economically costly variations to normal climate expectations, these events also created conditions around the world, which spawned extensive flooding, extended drought conditions and widespread wildfires.

TOWARDS DISASTER REDUCTION

In all of these cases the drama of the disasters and the urgent international activities to provide emergency relief assistance, command the attention of the international media – generally only for a few days. The consequences of the disasters last much longer and are more poignantly measured in solitude: lives lost, livelihoods disrupted, property destroyed and often increasingly fragile environments damaged. All of these losses impede the development of the human condition and often sacrifice previously hard-won individual and national accomplishments. They also compromise both immediate and long-term resources upon which current societies, as well as future generations, depend.

The subject of disaster and risk reduction draws its relevance from earlier contributions and previous practices in the disaster management fields, where traditionally the focus has been on preparedness for response. Those closest to affected populations – political authorities, professionals from many different fields, commercial interests, public organisations, educational institutions and local community leaders are increasingly recognising the essential public value of sustained efforts to reduce the social, economic and environmental costs of natural disasters. There has, for example, been a tidal change in the understanding of countries in Central America over the past three years, following the repeated devastating effects of natural disasters. There is now increased emphasis placed on risk, and an acceptance that disaster, development and environmental problems are inextricably linked.

Disaster reduction policies and measures need to be implemented, with a twofold aim: to enable societies to be resilient to natural hazards while ensuring that development efforts do not increase vulnerability to these hazards.

This understanding is essential if communities are to become more resilient to the effects of hazards so that disaster losses can be reduced in coming years. These activities make the news much less often, perhaps because they are mostly concerned with people during their ordinary work, focused on incorporating risk awareness into their daily existence.

Taking these developments into account, during the past 50 years, there has been a continuous evolution in the common understanding and practice of disaster management. To different political constituencies or various professional interests at particular times, there have been many different approaches to addressing catastrophic circumstances from natural hazards and their impacts on societies. These bodies of practice have variously been known as emergency assistance, disaster response, humanitarian assistance, civil defence, civil protection, homeland security and disaster prevention.

Currently, a more holistic approach focussing on risk and vulnerability has brought about the concept of risk reduction or disaster risk management. There is no doubt that the role of relief assistance during the acute phase of a crisis will remain important and need to be enhanced at all levels. However, the question must be asked: Can modern societies afford to value their social and material assets only after they have been lost in a disaster? In many places political commitment and the allocation of resources to address hazardous conditions have been concentrated overwhelmingly on shortterm emergency contingencies. Much greater attention will need to be given to protective strategies that can contribute to saving lives and protecting property and resources before they are lost.

From 1990 to 1999, during the International Decade for Natural Disaster Reduction (IDNDR) proclaimed by the General Assembly of the United Nations, work was done to advance a wider commitment to activities that could reduce the consequences of natural disasters, under the theme Building a Culture of Prevention. The Yokohama Strategy and Plan of Action for a Safer World stressed that every country had the sovereign and primary responsibility to protect its people, infrastructure and national social or economic assets from the impact of natural disasters. Experience gained since then has demonstrated that by focusing on the socio-economic factors involved, human actions can reduce vulnerability of societies to natural hazards and related technological and environmental disasters.

Initially, the *IDNDR* was influenced by largely scientific and technical interest groups. However, a broader global awareness of the social and economic consequences of natural disasters developed as the decade progressed, highlighting the increasing importance of engaging a much broader community in hazard awareness and risk management practices. The importance given to socio-economic vulnerability as a rapidly increasing factor of risk in most of today's societies underlined the need to encourage the wider participation of local communities in hazard and risk reduction activities.

> "We, the States Members of the United Nations and other States, having met at the World Conference on Natural Disaster Reduction, in the city of Yokohama, Japan, from 23 May to 27 May 1994, in partnership with non-governmental organisations, and with the participation of international organisations, the scientific community, business, industry and the media, deliberating within the framework of the International Decade for natural Disaster Reduction, expressing our deep concern for the continuing human suffering and disruption of development caused by natural disasters, and inspired by the Yokohama Strategy and Plan of

Action for a Safer World...." ...."adopted the following Principles, Strategy and Plan for Action"

1. Risk assessment is a required step for the adoption of adequate and successful disaster reduction policies and measures.
2. Disaster prevention and preparedness are of primary importance in reducing the need for disaster relief.
3. Disaster prevention and preparedness should be considered integral aspects of development policy and planning at national, regional, bilateral, multilateral and international levels.
4. The development and strengthening of capacities to prevent, reduce and mitigate disasters is a top priority area to be addressed so as to provide a strong basis for follow-up activities to the IDNDR.
5. Early warnings of impending disasters and their effective dissemination are key factors to successful disaster prevention and preparedness.
6. Preventive measures are most effective when they involve participation at all levels from the local community through the national government to the regional and international level.
7. Vulnerability can be reduced by the application of proper design and patterns of development focused on target groups by appropriate education and training of the whole community.
8. The international community accepts the need to share the necessary technology to prevent, reduce and mitigate disaster.
9. Environmental protection as a component of sustainable development consistent with poverty alleviation is imperative in the prevention and mitigation of natural disasters.

10. Each country bears the primary responsibility for protecting its people, infrastructure, and other national assets from the impact of natural disasters. The international community should demonstrate strong political determination required to make efficient use of existing resources, including financial, scientific and technological means, in the field of natural disaster reduction, bearing in mind the needs of the developing countries, particularly the least developed countries.

Natural disasters continue to strike and increase in magnitude, complexity, frequency and economic impact. Whilst the natural phenomena causing disasters are in most cases beyond human control, vulnerability is generally a result of human activity. Therefore, society must recognize and strengthen traditional methods and explore new ways to live with such risk, and take urgent actions to prevent as well as to reduce the effects of such disasters. The capacities to do so are available.

Although articulated in 1994, the principles contained in the Yokohama Strategy and Plan of Action for a Safer World are possibly more relevant to risk reduction now than when they were conceived.

DISASTER RISK REDUCTION STRATEGIES

Governments and communities must understand that disaster reduction policy is a wise investment. Direction and resource allocations often need to be provided from higher levels of authority within a society, as much as decisions and individual commitment need to grow from the local understanding and active participation of those people most immediately affected by disaster risks.

Where governments have not done so already, there is a need to regain a level of wide and inclusive national participation, before a disaster occurs. This public responsibility will require a collective discipline that can be sustained through the education and practice of many trades and professions.

Since disaster reduction is based on a continuous strategy of vulnerability and risk assessment, many actors need to be involved, drawn from governments, technical and educational institutions, professions, commercial interests and local communities. Their activities will need to be integrated into planning and development strategies that both enable and encourage the widespread exchange of information. New multidisciplinary relationships are essential if disaster reduction is to be both comprehensive and sustainable.

Vulnerability to disasters should be considered in a broad context encompassing specific human, social/cultural, economic, environmental and political dimensions, that relate to inequalities, gender relations and ethical and racial divisions. A disaster with all its negative consequences offers a good opportunity to formulate forward-looking policy concepts pertaining to social development and equity, economic growth, environmental quality and justice, i.e. sustainability.

However, to be successful, the integration of holistic disaster reduction strategies into development policies should happen from the outset, thereby solving a broad range of social, economic and environmental problems as well. This requires the participation of all relevant sectors (such as environment, finance, industry, transport, construction, agriculture, education and health). It also requires different forms of management than in the case of emergency or disaster management. The responsibilities of risk reduction are even more broadly extended than is commonly understood.

This is why the most efficient forms of hierarchical "command and control" practices for crisis management are much less suited to the deliberate and more widely considered forms of public, private and professional participation in risk reduction which draw their information and inspiration from many different sources in a society.

Disaster reduction strategies include, first and foremost, vulnerability and risk assessment, as well as a number of institutional capacities and operational abilities. The assessment of the vulnerability of critical facilities, social and economic infrastructure, the use of effective early warning systems, and the application of many different types of scientific, technical, and other skilled abilities are essential features of a disaster reduction strategy.

The sharing of information and experience, both for the purposes of public information and all forms of education and professional training are as important for creating a safety culture, as are the crucial involvement of local community action and new forms of partnership motivated by cooperation and shared responsibilities.

Fortunately, modern forms of information access and communications can facilitate the wider exposure and networking that these new and shifting forms of association require. Above all, despite these many contributions, functions associated with disaster reduction need to be viewed not as an expense, but as an investment in a society's future.

As common as all of these attributes are to any sustained strategy of disaster reduction, one must also take account of the various political, cultural, and social distinctions that exist among all countries. There are fundamental elements in every disaster reduction strategy, but the priorities, relative emphasis, available resources, and specific ways of implementation must take account of practices that are most suited tc local conditions, understanding and effectiveness.

Political Support for Disaster Risk Reduction

Political support for disaster risk reduction has to be established from the apex of political power but that can only be realistic if the perceptions of risk and the actions proposed accord with the cultural beliefs and habits of society. In today's interconnected world, societies are confronted with rapid winds of change. Therefore, the value of disaster risk reduction can only be realised through rigorous identification and continuous evaluation of the relationships that exist between the distinctive beliefs and human conditions in which people live, the changing environment people inhabit and depend upon for their livelihoods, and the immutable forces of nature. Most importantly, disaster risk reduction relies upon the consequences of collective decisions made and individual actions taken – or not taken.

The emergence of a disaster reduction culture is conditioned by contexts and processes that are described below:

— The sustainable development context, the ultimate international goal;

— The political context, essential for action;

— The three contexts linked to the pillars of sustainable development:

  (a) The socio-cultural system

  (b) The economic system

  (c) The environmental system.

Sustainability means recognising and making best use of the interconnection between social, economic and environmental goals to reduce significant hazard risks. This entails the ability to reduce one's exposure to, and recover from, infrequent large-scale, but also frequent smaller scale, natural and human driven events.

The bottom line for any country, especially the poorest, is to build sustainable communities thriving from generation to generation with a social foundation that provides for health, respects cultural diversity, is equitable and considers the needs of future generations. They require has a healthy and diverse ecological system that is life-sustaining and productive, a healthy and diverse economy that adapts to change and recognises social and ecological limits. This cannot be achieved without the incorporation of disaster reduction strategies, one of the six principles of sustainability supported by a strong political commitment.

Disaster risk management and reduction are about looking beyond hazards alone to consider prevailing conditions of vulnerability. It is the social, cultural, economic, and political setting in a country that makes people vulnerable to unfortunate events. The basis of this understanding is simple: the national character and chosen form of governance can be as much of a determinant in understanding the risks in a given country, as are the various social, economic and environmental determinants.

> "While we cannot do away with natural hazards, we can eliminate those we cause, minimise those we exacerbate, and reduce our vulnerability to most. Doing this requires healthy and resilient communities and ecosystems. Viewed in this light, disaster mitigation is clearly part of a broader strategy of sustainable development-making communities and nations socially, economically, and ecologically sustainable."
>
> —*J. Abramovitz*

The motivation to invest in disaster risk reduction is first and foremost a human, people centred concern. It is about improving standards of safety and living conditions with an eye on protection from hazards to increase resilience of communities. A safer society to withstand disasters may be argued as a case of ethics and social justice and equity. It is also motivated by economic gains.

Socio-economic development is seriously challenged when scarce funds are diverted from longer-term development objectives to shortterm emergency relief and reconstruction needs. It is considered by some as illusory to quantify benefits from disaster reduction. They see the issue foremost as a human and social concern rather than based on economic rationale and efficiency. Others advocate that effective planning and development options can only be based on a careful estimation of the economic gains and poverty impacts of disasters, accompanied by economic justification for the required investments in vulnerability reduction.

Environmentally unsound practices, global environmental changes, population growth, urbanisation, social injustice, poverty, and short-term economic vision are producing vulnerable societies. The impact of development on disasters should be fully embraced if disaster risk reduction is to yield its expected benefits. "Instead of demonising hazards for their impacts on society, it would be probably more correct to demonise society for its impacts on hazards!".

Sustainable Development and Poverty Reduction Initiatives

The escalation of severe disasters is increasingly posing a threat to both sustainable development and poverty reduction initiatives. As a consequence principle 1 of the Rio Declaration is imperilled. This states that human beings are at the centre of concerns for sustainable development and are entitled to a healthy and productive life in harmony with nature. Repeated exposure to disasters can lead to a downward spiral of poverty.

It is still the post-disaster reconstruction period that provides the most opportune time to introduce disaster reduction into sustainable development planning. Therefore, political commitment and social acceptance of the value of risk reduction are necessary for forward-looking developers who want to increase the sustainability of communities.

When perceived as a distinct set of activities, risk management initiatives are placed in competition with other developmental objectives, rather than being seen as integral parts of the same whole.

Political commitment is an essential quality for sustained efforts of risk reduction. Only political willingness can give disaster reduction the place it deserves. Obtaining political commitment from public authorities is one of the four overriding objectives of ISDR to effectively reduce the impacts of disasters.

This objective needs to be addressed through increased coordination at all levels, risk management strategies and the allocation of appropriate resources including development of new funding mechanisms. Disaster reduction should be dealt with as a policy issue across relevant fields of government including health, agriculture and environment.

To be feasible, disaster reduction needs to show it is able to address short-term and immediate needs of survival as well as to take care of longer-term objectives of prevention and capacity building. This approach is illustrated by efforts undertaken in the cities of *Manizales* and Medellin in Colombia.

There, the death toll and economic damage due to landslides and floods have decreased considerably thanks to initiatives undertaken by the municipalities, together with universities, the private sector and community groups, through reforestation, plant cover works, improved drainage systems and engineering works. In some cases, these investments are even generating income through harvesting and tourism.

Political change, economic reform and development of public policy to protect people and resources are fundamental solutions to treating causes rather than only symptoms. Politicians that undertake no-regret policies and apply precautionary principles in matters of environmental protection should be able to take the same stance regarding disaster reduction.

Similarly, the public that exercises great pressure to bring about environmental policy changes should become a political force putting pressure on governments to protect people from disasters. If it becomes a popular issue, disaster risk reduction will gain momentum. While disaster reduction will not reign without political willingness, a word should also be said about the negative consequences political decisions can have on disaster impacts. For example, huge hydraulic projects may change landscape references of communities and their perception of risk, thereby increasing vulnerability by reducing the people's capacity to assess and anticipate hazard-related threats.

Pillars of Sustainable Development

Socio-cultural context

The links between disaster and the socio-cultural system are an important component in disaster risk reduction and a pillar of sustainable development. The term culture is understood in a myriad of ways and represents an extremely complex notion. It is, therefore, useful to provide a definition.

Differences exist among groups of people, and these differences reflect a variety of factors including language, socio-economic and political systems, religion and ethnicity as well as historical experience and relationships towards nature. Each cultural group has its own set of experiences and expectations. Furthermore, relationships between people and groups of different cultures are often embedded in different sets of values, unequal power relations with some groups becoming dominant and others being marginalised. All of these factors are highly relevant in the context of natural disasters.

Much early thinking about disasters was based on a notion of nature and culture being separate. Disasters were seen as the products of a precocious and unpredictable nature and therefore to be out of the control of humans or referred to in terms such as acts of supernatural forces, or acts of god.

It became increasingly obvious that the causes of disasters are complex and that beside nature people are a causal factor. Looking beyond beliefs, more and more disasters are understood in terms of their cultural and social components. Vast differences in disaster vulnerability among countries and within individual societies have their roots in unequal sets of power relations, leading to unequal distribution and access to wealth among different cultures or political settings. It is important that ownership of the disaster context is not stripped from local people who can be left even more powerless than would be the case if external intervention did not occur. There is a growing appreciation of the need for disaster reduction activities to be based on more attentive participatory approaches involving local communities as much as possible, considering them as proactive stakeholders and not passive targets for intervention.

Common sense solutions in one cultural setting are often contrary to what may be common sense in others. Local socio-political structures and cultural conditions such as kinship arrangements, customary rights, community and family networks and systems of leadership nearly always persist during disasters and it is important that these are not undermined. For example, it is important to recognise that dealing with death and illness is a strong cultural process. Where decisions about matters such as mass burials are imposed on cultural groups by others, serious problems can occur that disrupt grieving and have long-term social, legal and psychological consequences.

The differing needs and roles of men and women also need to be taken into account. Men are usually seen as income generators while women ensure social cohesion and continuity by taking care of children, the elderly and the disabled. Different priorities, perceptions and abilities to cope with abnormal situations need careful thinking to maximise the success of risk management and to achieve sustainable development.

In many cultures, attachment to place is a critically important element, thus decisions to move people must be made carefully. In some cases, people have felt more afraid and at risk in the sites they have been moved to than if they had remained (even where the risk of death is relatively high). In many cases people are also unwilling to leave a house in which they have invested most of their time and money and which constitutes their principal legacy to their children.

In other instances, host communities have felt imposed upon by those who have been relocated and violent responses are not uncommon. The issue is that relocation of communities at risk may be scientifically the most attractive and reasonable prevention measure but it can be strongly opposed culturally.

Cultural change is an important consideration in disaster reduction as is cultural continuity. For example, intercommunity cooperation following disasters was extremely common among traditional Pacific island communities, and to a large extent sustained by ceremonial exchange systems. These exchange networks fell away as commercial trading, often centred in colonial capitals, replaced traditional forms of exchange, colonial governments replaced traditional political networks and missionaries discouraged exchanges as threats to Christianity. Relief aid also reduced the need to sustain such networks. However, with the migration of many Pacific islanders to places such as Australia, California and New Zealand, new exchange networks have emerged. Following disasters, major flows of resources now enter Pacific island states in the form of remittances from kinfolk. Culturally, disasters have become important events through which the Pacific island diasporas maintain links with the home islands.

An important finding of many researchers working in developing countries or in local communities is that a wide variety of measures for reducing disasters existed in earlier, often pre-colonial, times. A variety of socio-cultural or economic factors mentioned have gradually eroded these measures, undermining cultural support and social activities that might have contributed to sharing the exposure to risk among members of the community. The economic context

The links between disaster and the economic system, another pillar of sustainable development, are as clear as the financial incentive for disaster reduction. Indeed, historically people have always made investments to obtain, and then to protect, those resources that hold the greatest value for them. This is the principle behind insurance or other efforts to spread risk among a community including joint ownership or responsibility for protecting assets.

The concern demonstrated by a farmer to protect a single cow, or a fisherman to mend nets in subsistence economies, as well as the rapid growth investment in business continuity practices seen in more commercialised societies, validate the economic basis of reducing risks in order to minimise the negative impacts of future disasters. Economics and the awareness of the importance of disasters that increase in severity and frequency through human action, provide incentives for development banks and international assistance institutions to integrate risk reduction in their development strategies and to develop innovative forms of financial investment.

Risk management planning involves an estimation of the impacts of disasters on the economy, based on the best available hazard maps and macroeconomic data. These include assessments of the costs of disasters, evaluation of the costs and benefits of disaster reduction and risk transfer measures (including the value of improved forecasting systems) and incentives from the international community that lead towards proactive disaster reduction projects. Such studies are carried out through international cooperative arrangements.

Given the recurrence and frequency of natural hazards, a concerted effort will always be required to respond effectively to them, and to assess the frequency of emergency recovery assistance, as well as the prospects of reducing damage in the future.

The benefits of long-term disaster management versus the costs of repeated short-term post-disaster reconstruction need to be documented. In view of the exorbitant economic and social costs of recurring disasters, long-term hazard reduction planning is, more and more, a guiding principle and prerequisite for the sustainability of physical investments in need of replacement, reconstruction or construction.

Improvement in, and enforcement of, regulatory frameworks of disaster reduction including disaster-related insurance, building codes and land use planning will ensure that infrastructure is properly sited and built to minimise damages as well as to reduce the costs of repair. This involves public insurance policy, market and regulatory incentives for risk and vulnerability reduction, protection protection against fluctuations in insurance/re-insurance prices, augmentation of insurance coverage at reasonable cost and backstop financial mechanisms.

The relationship between disaster and risk reduction and globalisation also needs to be researched further to explore, on the one hand the detrimental effects of deregulation and economic interconnection, and on the other hand, the beneficial effects associated with trade opportunities and economic competitiveness.

In a globalising world, the potential of risk reduction as an essential element to building competitiveness, protecting investment and securing trade opportunities, while ensuring that new risks are not created and business not interrupted, has to be fully comprehended.

Environmental context

The third system with which disaster reduction is closely

linked is the environmental system, yet another pillar of sustainable development. Disasters do not only affect the built environment but also the natural environment. Furthermore, environmental degradation increases the intensity of natural hazards and is often the factor that transforms the hazard, or climatic extreme such as a heavy downpour, into a disaster. For example, river and lake floods are aggravated or even caused by deforestation which causes erosion and clogs rivers. Poverty and hazard vulnerability is integrally linked to this situation. The poor are compelled to exploit environmental resources for survival, therefore increasing both risk and exposure to disasters, in particular those triggered by floods, drought and landslides.

The natural environment provides solutions to increase protection against disaster impacts. Therefore, successful disaster reduction should enhance environmental quality, which includes protection of natural resources and open space, management of water run-off, and reduction of pollution.

Successful environmental policies should highlight the effectiveness of disaster reduction measures. This should entail an acceptance of some degree of natural disturbance to avoid the greater consequences of extreme events, and an appraisal of alternative solutions to an exclusively engineering approach. There is growing recognition that by following principles of wise environmental management, increased hazard protection as well as economic benefits can be provided by the natural environment. This can be accomplished by building national and local capacities, exchanging experience and information regionally and engaging programme and investment partners internationally.

The wealth of information and knowledge from both environmental and disaster management studies should be mutually beneficial. Both areas are inherently multi-disciplinary and dynamic in their approach and analysis of the socio-environmental nexus. Institutionally, both have been, and largely continue to be, operated by the public sector and NGOs. Similar tools are continuously being refined in both fields, namely vulnerability indexing, inventory mechanisms, educational programmes for public awareness and impact assessments.

Encompassing long-term comprehensive goals to manage growth, development and land use implies incorporating an effective environmental component into disaster reduction strategies. Adapted, sustainable and integrated management of natural resources, including reforestation schemes, proper land use and judicious settlements should increase the resilience of communities to disasters by reversing current trends of environmental degradation and dealing with hazard management in a comprehensive way. Secondary benefits expected from the introduction of environmental projects in disaster reduction programmes include social acceptance, political feasibility and economic rationale.

Disaster reduction and environmental management should become national priorities. Entities responsible for disaster reduction should have clear environmental mandates. Coordinated and inter-agency programmes are needed to promote a holistic problem-solving strategy, justifying the protection and restoration of natural functions of ecosystems, and assessing programme subsidies to create the right incentives for sustainability. Environmental accounting systems that produce information suited for decision-making should reflect disaster reduction considerations. Additional studies are needed to improve systems of ecological economic accounting. Translating environmental resources and services into conventional economic figures is still very much a challenge.

As disaster reduction and environment have a lot in common, the disaster reduction community should look closely at experience gained in promoting environmental policies. The environmental community has been promoting its agenda for 30 years. Today, the role of environmental strategies to achieve sustainable development is now no longer questioned and disaster reduction policy must follow a similar path.

Until recently, the relationship between environmental degradation and mismanagement, hazard incidence and vulnerability was a non-issue in most regions and countries except for lip-service. Neither the subject nor the designated authorities for disaster management were thought to be relevant for ecologists and environmentalists. There was little discussion, and even less organisational contact, linking the perceived interests of environmental management and the dynamics associated with risk reduction.

In fact, the primary actors frequently considered one another to be antagonists, struggling to represent forces either empowering the interests of the people or expanding the uncompromising power and authority of the State, often played out over competing uses of land and natural resources. It should also be recalled that the existence of environmental divisions in bilateral and multilateral agencies as well as of environmental ministries was not the norm during the 1980s.

This changed dramatically in the closing years of the 1990s in Latin America and the Caribbean. El Niño and Hurricanes Georges and Mitch focused attention on the importance of the full range of the hydrological cycle to both development and disaster concerns. The magnitude of the resulting fires, drought, flooding and landslides associated with these disasters inevitably stimulated discussion about the relationships that exist between environmental mismanagement and the occurrence of hazards.

6

Risk Awareness and Assessment

Awareness of risk is therefore a necessary condition to engage in disaster risk reduction. The focus on risk management, rather than on the disaster event, reflects a proactive attitude for dealing with potential threats to social and materials assets, before they are lost. Understanding risk relates to the ability to define what could happen in the future, given a range of possible alternatives to choose from. Assessing risks, based on vulnerability and hazard analysis, is a required step for the adoption of adequate and successful disaster reduction policies and measures.

Levels of risk awareness depend largely upon the quantity and quality of available information and on the difference in people's perceptions of risk. People are more vulnerable when they are not aware of the hazards that pose a threat to their lives and assets. Risk awareness varies among people, communities, agencies and governments, according to their particular perceptions. These can be influenced by the knowledge of hazards and vulnerabilities, as well as by the availability of accurate and timely information about them.

Two elements are essential in the formulation of risk: the probability of occurrence for a given threat – hazard;

and the degree of susceptibility of the element exposed to that source—vulnerability. The negative impact, or the disaster, will depend on the characteristics, probability and intensity of the hazard, as well as the susceptibility of the exposed elements based on physical, social, economic and environmental conditions.

The recognition of vulnerability as a key element in the risk equation has also been accompanied by a growing interest in linking the positive capacities of people to cope, withstand and recover from the impact of hazards. It conveys a sense of the potential for managerial and operational capabilities to reduce the extent of hazards and the degree of vulnerability.

Social dimensions are intimately linked to the decision-making process to deal with disaster risk, as they embrace a range of risk perceptions and their underlying causes. A closer look at the nature of hazards and the notions of vulnerability and capacities in the context of disaster risk, allows for a better and more comprehensive understanding of the challenges posed by disaster risk reduction.

NATURE OF HAZARDS

Most natural hazards may be inevitable, disasters are not. By seeking to understand and to anticipate future hazards by study of the past and monitoring of present situations, a community or public authority is poised to minimise the risk of a disaster. It is a measure of people's wisdom and a society's values if a community is able to learn from the experiences of others, rather than to suffer its own. There is a wealth of knowledge about the nature and consequences of different hazards, expected frequency, magnitude and potential geographical impacts, but many fewer examples of lessons learned from them.

Hazards are increasingly dynamic and with highly varying potential impacts. Due to changing environments, many countries and regional organisations call for a greater knowledge of hazard characteristics. Such knowledge requires additional, more focussed research on hazards and a greater understanding of their nature, effects and history.

A wide range of geophysical, meteorological, hydrological, environmental, technological, biological and even socio-political hazards, alone or in complex interaction, can threaten living and sustainable development. Hazards have often been divided into natural, humaninduced technological and increasingly negative effects of environmental degradation is being added to this list.

While natural hazards can be divided into three broad categories—hydrometeorological, geological and biological—the variety, geographical coverage and types of impacts are huge. Forest fires, for example, are recognised as a natural hazard but are often referred to as environmental, along with pest infestation and desertification. In order to distinguish between different hazard types, many institutions have developed hazard catalogues.

The strong compound relation between different types of natural hazards may give the impression that attempts to catalogue them are fatuous. At what stage does a landslide, recognised as a geological hazard, becomes a mudflow, which is often classified as a hydrological hazard? In the same vein, primary hazards often give rise to a myriad of related potential collateral or secondary hazards. In many cases, these cause greater threat to a community than do the primary hazards. Tropical cyclones can trigger other hazards, in particular storm surges, flash foods and landslides. Often the most serious impact of a tropical cyclone comes from the associated coastal and river floods. Similarly, damages related to earthquakes are often caused by landslides, fires, tsunamis, and floods.

All communities – urban or rural – are vulnerable to most hazards. However, different regions will be more prone to certain types of hazards than others. Floods and windstorms are the hazards that most frequently lead to disasters in Asia, the Pacific, Europe and North America, while it is droughts and epidemics that are reported in African countries. In contrast, Pacific and Caribbean islands are most vulnerable to the effects of tropical cyclones. El Niño events, floods, volcanic eruptions and earthquakes affect in greater degree the Andean and Meso-American countries. Even within a specific region, such as the Pacific, the frequency and intensity of specific hazards varies from one country to another. Hydrometeorological hazards are most common and floods alone account for two-thirds of people affected by natural hazards.

In the same way, different levels of income groups are more or less vulnerable to certain types of hazards. While droughts affect primarily the lower social classes, the impact of earthquakes and floods are more evenly spread out between society.

NATURE OF VULNERABILITY AND CAPACITY

Over the past fifty years there has been a significant and important development in the understanding about what makes people, social, economic and environmental assets susceptible to hazards. The concept of vulnerability may have been referred to first by engineers, in considering construction values and building designs related to levels of resistance to physical forces exerted by earthquakes, wind and water. During the 1980s and 1990s, there was a growing interest in the linkages between disasters and development. Originally focussed on considering primarily the impact of disaster on development, it was then expanded also to address the impact of development on the toll of disaster related damage. This expressed a new range of socio-economic and environmental concerns built around the notion of vulnerability.

In parallel with this expanded interest on the relationship between disasters and development during the last decades, the role of community participation as well as people's general coping capacities was also recognized as key elements in explaining disaster risk. The creative link between the negative conditions with which people live, and the often overlooked positive attributes which they also possess, underline the importance of socio-economic dimensions of risk. However, it remains a challenge to encourage the identification of locally available strengths and capacities to reduce risk to hazards. The importance of exposing capacities hidden in non-disaster times becomes a critical task for disaster risk reduction. Capacity apply to all levels of society and social organisations, and a broad range of physical, social, economic and ecological considerations.

Vulnerability is a reflection of the state of the individual and collective physical, social, economic and environmental conditions at hand that are shaped continually by attitudinal, behavioural, cultural, socio-economic and political influences at the individuals, families, communities, and countries. Governed by human activity, vulnerability cannot be isolated from ongoing development efforts, and it therefore plays a critical role in the social, economic and ecological spheres of sustainable development.

The following four broad areas in which different aspects of vulnerability can be grouped. They are depicted by intersecting circles to show that all spheres interact with one another.

— *Physical factors*: This concept is conventionally asset-oriented, and comes from the schools of land use planning, engineering and architecture. Physical aspects of vulnerability, although continually broadening in scope, still mainly refer to the location considerations and susceptibilities of the built environment. It may be described as exposure to hazards – "living in harms ways" or "being in the wrong place at the wrong time." Physical vulnerability may be determined by aspects such as density levels, remoteness of a settlement, its siting, design and materials used for critical infrastructure and for housing.

— *Social factors*: Social vulnerability is linked to the level of well being of individuals, communities and society. It includes aspects related to levels of literacy and education, the existence of peace and security, access to basic human rights, systems of good governance, social equity, positive traditional values, knowledge structures, customs and ideological beliefs, and overall collective organisational systems.

Some groups are more vulnerable than others, mainly those less privileged in class and caste structures, ethnic minorities, the very young and very old, and other disadvantaged and marginalised segments of the population. Gender issues, particularly the role of women, are also important. In many societies, women have a primary responsibility for domestic life, essential shelter and basic needs. Therefore, women are more likely to become more burdened, or more vulnerable in times of crisis.

Public health, concerning physical, mental and psychological well being, is a critical aspect of social vulnerability. The disabled, of whom there are hundreds of millions world-wide, are particularly susceptible, as their evacuation and continued care is severely hampered during disasters. Predisposition to infection, exaggerated exposure to communicable diseases, lack of defensive mechanisms, insufficient basic infrastructure, especially water supply and sanitation, as well as inadequate health care facilities and supplies, are all expressions of increased vulnerability.

Levels of literacy and training, traditional knowledge systems, and access to information on disaster risk and measures, as well cultural aspects, such as indigenous beliefs, traditions and ways of coping also shape levels of susceptibility. Deeply rooted beliefs that are destiny oriented or pose a fatalistic vision of disasters, can reflect a religious or ideologically inherited sense of vulnerability, and these people may present a great challenge in moving towards the acceptance of a culture of prevention and protection.

Social vulnerability is also linked with other factors, like the state of domination and power relations in the concerned society. A great social cohesion and regulation improves the coping capacities, whereas social insecurity increases vulnerability. In this sense, the decline of traditional structures, civic groups or communities formerly engaged in the collective well being, or in the protection of the weakest people, can strengthen the disastrous consequences of a hazard. Organisational and governance structures play an important role in the level of social vulnerability.

— *Economic factors*: Levels of vulnerability are highly dependent upon the economic status of individuals, communities and nations. The poor are in general far more vulnerable than economically better people of society. This relates both to the proportional possibility of higher losses when a disaster strikes, and to the capacity to recover from disasters. The links between the eradication of poverty, impact consequences on recovery conditions from natural disasters, and the state of the environmental resource base upon which both depend are crucial.

  Economic vulnerability also includes levels of individual, community and national economic reserves, levels of debt and the degree of access to credit and loans as well as insurance. An economy lacking in diversity is generally more vulnerable. Similarly, inadequate access to critical and basic socio-economic infrastructure, including communication networks, utilities and supplies, transportation, water, sewage and health care facilities increase people's exposure to risk.

— *Ecological factors*: The discussion of environmental aspects of vulnerability covers a very broad range of issues in the interacting social, economic and ecological aspects of sustainable development as it relates to disaster risk reduction. The key aspects of environmental vulnerability can be summarised by the following five distinctions:

  — The extent of natural resource depletion.

  — The state of resource degradation.

  — Loss of resilience of the ecological systems.

— Loss of biodiversity.
— Exposure to toxic and hazardous pollutants.

Trends in Disaster Impact

le no country in the world is entirely safe, lack of capacity to limit the impact of hazards remains a major burden for developing countries, where more than 90 per cent of natural disaster related deaths are to be found. Twenty-four of the 49 least developed countries (LDCs) still face high levels of disaster risk. At least six of them have been hit by between two and eight major disasters per year in the last 25 years, with long-term consequences for human development. These figures do not include the consequences of the many smaller and unrecorded disasters that cause significant loss at the local community level.

The re-insurance giant Munich Re, a member of the ISDR Inter-agency Task Force, in its annual publication Topics for 2000, looked at the trend of economic losses and insurance costs over a 50 year period linked to what it calls "great natural catastrophes".

There were 20 of these, costing the world US$ 38 billion (at 1998 values) between 1950 and 1959. However, between 1990 and 1999, there were 82 such major disasters and the economic losses had risen to a total of US$ 535 billion. That is, disasters had multiplied fourfold but economic losses were 14 times higher. And in each decade between, both the number of great disasters and the economic loss involved had risen steadily. However, losses in 2000 and 2001 were down.

These are absolute figures of economic loss, most of them to be found in developed and industrialised countries. But seen as losses by percentage of GDP, it is developing countries that lose most in relative terms, as shown in the graphic based on figures provided by

Munich Re. For example, the economic losses of the United States from the 1997-98 El Niño event were estimated to US$ 1.96 billion or 0.03 per cent of GDP. The economic losses in Ecuador were US$ 2.9 billion, but this represented 14.6 per cent of GDP.

The International Federation of Red Cross and Red Crescent Societies, another ISDR Task Force member, confirms the worsening trend of human suffering and economic loss during the last decade. The total number of people each year affected by natural disaster – that is, who at least for a time either lost their homes, their crops, their animals, their livelihoods, or their health, because of the disaster – almost doubled between 1990 and 1999, by an average of 188 million people per year. This is six times more than the average of 31 million people affected annually by conflict.

Comparing the last three decades, the trend shows an increase in the number of natural hazard events and of affected populations. Even though the number of disasters has more than tripled since the 1970s, the reported death toll has decreased to less than half. This is among other factors due to improved early warning systems and increased preparedness. This statistic varies enormously depending on region and figures used. One needs to bear in mind that large disasters are rare events that defeat any statistical analysis in the short term. Perhaps more significant in the life of many are those daily disasters, generally under-reported and not reflected at all in global figures on losses, but accumulating to probably large tolls of both economic and health losses.

There is a considerable geographic variation in the occurrence and impact of natural hazards. Asia is disproportionately affected with approximately 43 per-cent of all natural disasters in the last decade. During the same period, Asia accounted for almost 70 per cent of all lives lost due to natural hazards. During the two El Niño years of 1991-92 and 1997-98, floods in China alone affected over 200 million people in each year. Nevertheless, in relative terms and counted per capita, Africa is the most heavily affected country, in particular when drought, epidemics and famine are included.

The single most terrible year in human loss during the last decade was 1991, when a cyclone devastated Bangladesh killing 139,000 people, bringing the global total of deaths for that year to 200,000. Cyclones are cyclical events and they continue to hit the Bangladesh coasts but no such catastrophe has happened again. This is at least in part because the machinery of warning and preparedness – watchful officials, an aware public and a stronger sense of community responsibility – came into play.

The worst global economic loss during last decade occurred in 1995, due to the Great Hanshin-Awaji earthquake in Kobe, Japan. A highly developed, prepared and economically strong nation faced serious set backs economically by loosing important facilities of its primary port. Even seven years after that disaster, the amount of shipping trade in Kobe has dropped by 15 percent. But now Kobe is rebuilt and modernised.

TRENDS IN HAZARDS

Until recently, the intensity and frequency of natural hazards, as events, whether geological or hydrometeorological in nature, only varied on very long time-scales due to natural variation in global temperatures and variation in the intensity of seismic activity.

Today, in particular hydrometeorological hazards are increasing due to human activities. The findings of the Intergovernmental Panel on Climate Change (IPCC) provide a new outlook about the changing patterns related to hazards themselves. Certainly, the scale of volcanic or seismic activity is not altered by human-induced sources, but it appears that our changing climate is affecting both the frequency and intensity of hydrometeorological hazards and related mass movements. Although it is very difficult to show scientific evidence of these changes, projections for the future invite concern.

Volcanic Hazards

About 50 to 60 volcanoes erupt every year worldwide. Large eruptions endanger lives, human settlements and livelihoods of the almost 500 million people estimated to live near active volcanoes in 2000. That number will increase in the future as today more than 60 large cities are located near potentially active volcanoes, threatened by volcanic eruption.

Volcanoes with high activity are located predominantly in developing countries, particularly in Latin America, the Caribbean, parts of Asia and in the southwest Pacific. In these countries, despite the improvements in many national civil defence agencies' capacities to manage volcanic emergencies, eruptions are becoming increasingly risky because of rising population density and intense interweaving of infrastructure in the areas surrounding volcanoes.

As the physical characteristics and chemical properties of a specific volcano become better known, it can be more easily monitored. However, the prediction of an impending eruption can still remain a major challenge for volcanologists. Therefore, predicting future volcanic eruptions and related hazards must also be matched with a series of other forms of mitigation, including the following:

— Volcanic risk analysis.
— Early warning and short-term forecast of eruptions.
— Timely and effectively organised evacuation of people from hazardous areas.
— Development and application of land-use and contingency plans to minimise future volcanic disasters. Sustained information and educational programs for the population.

Major volcanic eruptions do not occur spontaneously and are preceded by a variety of physical, geological and chemical changes, which accompany the rise of magma toward the surface. The monitoring and measurement of these changes with well established scientific techniques provide the best opportunity to develop a warning system. Recent volcanic disasters show that the cost of monitoring volcanic activity and pre-disaster planning is very small when compared to the potential losses.

For early warning to be effective, sustained public education and information is necessary. This includes understanding results of volcanological studies and analysis, the possible dangers and the local plans to address them prior to the occurrence of emergency conditions. It can be done through the use of brochures, lectures, or courses although the best prepared communities also conduct regular disaster warning and prevention exercises.

In 1990, the International Association of Volcanology and Chemistry of the Earth's Interior (IAVCEI) launched a program to support the IDNDR and to promote the reduction of risks related to volcanoes. The initiative selected 16 volcanoes for monitoring and research with the aim of directing attention to a small number of active volcanoes, and to encourage the establishment of a range of research and public-awareness activities aimed at enhancing an understanding of the volcanoes and the hazards they pose.

That commitment demonstrated a concentrated effort within the scientific community to publicise the realistic aspects of disaster reduction by working in close association with communities at risk from volcanic hazards. Such collaborative scientific activities continue to show benefits as quite a lot of work continues with those same volcanoes. As a result of improvements in monitoring made during the IDNDR, better data has been developed, especially as those volcanoes continue to be restless. Ongoing work that would not have occurred were it not for this earlier concentrated attention includes, ongoing German- Indonesian cooperation at Merapi Volcano, on the Indonesian island of Java.

Climate Related Hazards

Societies are increasingly dependant on medium to long term variations in the climate, such as El Niño/La Niña, which affect precipitation and temperatures over time-scales of two to three years. These regional climatic shifts, the specific character of which is still very much unknown, develop their own variation in hazard trends, in particular hydro-climatic hazards associated with climate variability. The prevalence of droughts and floods as leading hazards shows that many countries are particularly vulnerable in dealing with current natural variability and extremes, let alone climate change.

The projected changes in climate will adversely affect many regions, in particular tropical and sub-tropical regions of the planet. When dealing with the complex issue of climate change there are some observations that can now be accepted as fact. It is now established that temperatures are increasing globally, although these increases are not evenly distributed around the planet.

As the atmosphere becomes warmer throughout the world it can absorb more water vapour, leading to a general increase in humidity. As a result there is the probability that tropical storms and cyclones will be accompanied by extreme precipitation increases.

Unfortunately, these factors have a compound effect on the occurrence and impact of disasters. On the one hand, they affect the intensity and frequency of extreme hydrometeorological events, and on the other hand, they increase the vulnerability of societies. As we know, change in precipitation patterns, soil moisture and vegetation cover, are linked to the occurrence of floods, droughts, but also landslides and debris flow events. Climate change is also resulting in slight sea level rise and may cause more devastating storms and hurricanes in coastal areas. The only natural hazards that are not directly influenced by climate change are, possibly, volcanic eruptions and earthquakes.

The Inter-Agency Task Force on Disaster Reduction (IATF/DR) of the ISDR has a working group dealing with climate and disasters and another with wildland fires. In the area of drought preparedness and mitigation, there are a number of coordinated and collaborative initiatives that are foreseen to be undertaken within the framework of the ISDR Task Force involving all its working groups.

Drought

Absence of a precise and universally accepted definition of drought adds to the confusion as to whether it exists, and if it does the degree of its severity. Thus, drought is often forgotten once it ends, and everybody seems to be caught unawares again by the next one. Most of the drought definitions have therefore been application (impact) specific. Other drought definitions have been regional specific. The discussions of drought here are focused on three types of drought – meteorological, agricultural, and hydrological. Meteorological drought is principally defined by the deficiency of precipitation from expected or normal levels over an extended period of time. Hydrological drought is best defined by deficiencies in surface and subsurface water supplies, leading to a lack of water for meeting normal and specific water demands. Agricultural drought may be characterised by deficiency in the water availability for specific agricultural operations such as deficiency of in soil moisture, which is one of the most critical factors in defining crop production potential.

During the coming decade and century, it is expected that drought vulnerability will increase, mainly due to development pressures, population increases, and environmental degradation that could itself lead to climate change. Several efforts have therefore been made at international, regional and national levels to address drought challenges. The international and regional efforts include the programmes and activities of the organisations such as WMO, FAO, WFP, IFAD, ADPC, ACMAD and the Drought Monitoring Centres in Africa, US/NOAA, IRI of Columbia University and USGS, that have established programmes to deal with drought monitoring, prediction, early warning and disaster preparedness. They are also covered by the work of the UN sustainable development conventions, the UNFCCC, UNCCD and CBD.

Drought, unlike sudden-onset disasters, has some unique characteristics that may require different approaches to effectively address how to reduce their impacts:

— Drought does not directly destroy food in storage, shelter or infrastructure.

— Its effects are cumulative.

— It is often very difficult to detect its onset until some major impacts such as lack of water or food become discernible.

— Impacts can be spread over a larger geographical area than the damages that result from most of the other natural disasters, and hence quantification of impacts and provision of disaster relief is far more difficult.

Further, there are several social and economic parameters that affect the severity of drought including food prices, wars, various intervention methods, human activity, vegetation, water supplies and demands, making it extremely difficult to quantify its severity and also provide universal definition and indicators of drought. Drought risk is a product of a region's exposure to the natural hazards and its vulnerability to extended periods of water shortage. To reduce serious consequences, affected nations must improve understandings of hazards and the factors that influence vulnerability, and establish comprehensive and integrated early warning systems.

Drought is the most common hazard in Zimbabwe, a country whose economy is dependent on agriculture. The incidence of drought is often linked to the occurrence of El Niño episodes and has worsened since the 1980s. Floods frequently occurring in the southern and northern provinces of the country compound drought conditions in other parts of the country. In 1996, there were localised floods resulting from abnormally heavy downpours. However, in 2000, flooding associated with Cyclone Eline caused considerable infrastructure and environmental damage in the country. The livelihoods of more than 250,000 people were affected in rural areas, with 100 fatalities and more than US$ 7.5 million in losses recorded.

Drought has been a recurrent feature in most parts of Southern Africa, with five major periods of drought since

1980: 1982-83, 1987-88, 1991- 92, 1994-95 and 1997-98. Three of these events were regional in scale, with the 1991-92 drought considered the "worst in living memory", placing more than 20 million people at serious risk.

The persistent multi year drought in Central and Southwest Asia is an example of climatic variability that has affected up to 60 million people in parts of Iran, Afghanistan, Tajikistan, Uzbekistan and Turkmenistan, since November 2001. Chronic political instability in many parts of the region and the recent military action in Afghanistan have further complicated the situation. A recent study by the International Research Institute for Climate Prediction (IRI) concludes that Central and Southwest Asia represent the largest region of persistent drought over the last three years in the world. In Iran alone, 37 million people are affected. Water reserves in the country were down by 45 percent in 2001, 800,000 heads of livestock were lost in 2000, and 2.6 million hectares of irrigated land and 4 million hectares of rain-fed agriculture were affected. Damage to agriculture and livestock has been estimated by the UN at US$ 2.5 billion in 2001 and US$ 1.7 billions in 2000. Afghanistan and Pakistan are affected on a similar scale.

Sea Level Rise and Coastal Systems

Coastal zones are characterised by much diversity of ecosystems and a variety of socio-economic activities. An estimated 46 million people per year, living in coastal areas, are at risk of flooding from storm surges, and sea-level rise. Climate change will exacerbate these trends with significant impact upon the ecosystems and populations. A growing number of people will, continue to be located in coastal areas. Many traditional communities and subsistence level populations also rely on the resource wealth of coastal areas and continue to be drawn to these higher risk coastal regions. For example, indigenous coastal and island communities in the Torres Strait of Australia and in New Zealand's Pacific Island Territories are especially vulnerable. Although adaptation options do exist, such measures are not easily implemented on low-lying land. Also, climate change and sea-level rise issues are not as yet well incorporated into current models and frameworks for coastal zone management. There is a direct link between tropical sea temperature in the oceans and the frequency of tropical cyclones, hurricanes or typhoons. More heat in the atmosphere means more evaporation which means more rainfall and more flooding in some places, more frequent drought in others, more violent windstorms or heavier snows elsewhere.

Environmental Degradation

As human activity continues to alter the biosphere, changes result in the environment in specific places and at ecosystem levels. Environmental degradation compounds the actual impact of disasters, limits an area's ability to absorb the impact, and lowers the overall general natural resilience to hazard impact and disaster recovery. In addition, environmental degradation that occurs and is significant enough to alter the natural patterns in an ecosystem, also affects the regular temporal and spatial occurrence of natural phenomenon. Climate change is currently the most obvious example.

The interconnectedness between environmental degradation and progressive impact of natural disasters can be illustrated by the case of the Yangtze River Basin, in China, where concerns related to environmental vulnerability have been incorporated in watershed management. Viet Nam offers another example of the complex links between deforestation and floods/ landslides. Viet Nam's forest cover dropped from 43 per cent to 28 percent in 50 years. This is due to a combination of many years of war, with the use of deforestation as a tool of war, legal and illegal trade in timber as Viet Nam's economy became more open to international investment and trade, and, it is also quite likely, climate change. Reduced forest cover will make the people of Viet Nam more vulnerable to floods and landslides.

Land Degradation and Flash Floods

According to UNEP data, two thirds of Africa is dry land over 70 percent of which is classified as degraded. About 90 per cent of pasture land and 85 percent of crop lands in the countries closest to the Sahara have been affected and there is some evidence that the desert is advancing towards the south and east. Deforestation is an important catalyst of land exhaustion and soil erosion. In Africa, more than 90 percent of all wood is used for cooking and other energy needs and the demand for fuel wood has grown considerably since the oil price rise in 1974. Since kerosene is expensive to buy, there is an urban shadow of stripped land around most settlements. In effect, economic and social pressures – made worse by drought – have caused the breakdown of the traditional system of land use which was adapted to this fragile environment. Flood risk, especially flash floods, is also exacerbated by increasing land degradation. In Southern Africa, escalating land degradation is strongly associated with overgrazing, which accounts for more than half the soil degradation in the region.

Technological Hazards

Technological hazards are related to quickly occurring, high-impact events such as hazardous spills and nuclear accidents, and are therefore more linked with exposure, than long-term environmental degradation. In the case of hazardous materials – chemical and toxic waste leakage – exposure is the critical factor. That was the case in Bhopal, India, in 1984, where material leaked to form a deadly cloud that killed and injured a huge number of people – most of whom came from poor families allowed to settle around the chemical plant. The fatal consequences of this chemical release were directly related to modernisation efforts introduced as a complex and poorly managed industrial production system into a society unable to cope with it.

A very important aspect of exposure to technological hazards is the fact that they are not exclusively confined to urban-industrial societies. Virtually every modern product and process is disseminated to most countries and social settings. Of 25 nations with operating nuclear power stations, at least 14 are in developing countries. Great oil spills and releases of nuclear radiation are associated with the dominant energy and transportation technologies. Chernobyl, Exxon Valdez, Minimata and Bophal, are some well known examples of technological disasters.

Biohazards and Vulnerability

HIV/AIDS can be considered a biological hazard. However, due to its enormous real and potential impact on the human community, it also constitutes a major vulnerability factor to the impact of other natural hazards. In particular, HIV/AIDS exacerbates vulnerability to drought conditions. Household size and income diversification, which count as key strategies to cope with droughts, are severely affected by HIV/AIDS, both by reducing the labour force and diverting vital economic resources towards medication and treatments. Moreover, infected people living in cities, usually return to their home villages to die, reinforcing the already higher vulnerability in rural environments in most African countries.

TRENDS IN PHYSICAL VULNERABILITY

Ninety percent of the global population growth is taking place in least developed countries (LDCs). In these countries, exposure to hazards is already high through dense concentrations of population in largely unsafe human settlements. Vulnerability levels are also exacerbated by socio-economic and environmental conditions. In 1980, sub-Saharan Africa had a population of 385 million. This figure is expected to at least double by 2005. Population growth is outstripping food production that represents 40 percent of GDP in some instances. But even this figure is precarious given less reliable rainfall patterns.

The long-term trends of demographic growth for LDCs are creating environmental, as well as political, refugees. As many as 10 million people have emigrated during recent years but there may eventually be even greater redistributions of the African population in response to the deteriorating food situation. Some of this redistribution will likely concentrate even greater numbers in hazardous areas.

Due to the urban concentration of population, the greatest potential for disaster exists in the hundred most populous cities. Over three-quarters of these are exposed to at least one natural hazard. No less than seventy of these cities can expect, on average, to experience a strong earthquake at least once every fifty years. The greatest concern is for the fifty fastest growing cities, all of which are located in developing countries. Cities were often founded on accessible locations with inherent risks such as coastlines, to facilitate transport or floodplains because of their fertility and ample space for growth. Urbanisation and increasing competition for land, results in the creation of unregulated construction which spills over into high risk areas, such as along hill sides, into low lying areas, next to industries, or on flood plains.

Cities now hold disproportionate amounts of material wealth in terms of both residential and commercial buildings and infrastructure. This infrastructure is critical to the functioning of the city. The impact of disasters on cities can devastate national economies and industrial markets at an international level. This is especially important true for nation states, or emerging economies, where one or perhaps two primary urban areas will account for the vast majority of economic and social activity.

The dynamic growth of coastal areas evident in the Andean sub-region is also seen elsewhere. Nearly 3 billion people live in coastal zones, and 13 of the 15 largest cities are also located on the sea. Not only is the exposure of people exacerbated by the occupation of hazard-prone areas, the concentration of industrial infrastructure and critical facilities are also affected. Communication networks and educational and health infrastructure are becoming more vulnerable to the potential impact of natural hazards.

Behind the rapid urbanisation process, rural displacement accounts for the rapid growth of informal, illegal settlements in the most dangerous places near cities like Mexico City, Rio de Janeiro and Manila, amongst others. Disaster risk concerns go hand in hand with other equally pressing urban issues, such as decaying infrastructure, poor housing and homelessness, hazardous industries, inadequate services, unaffordable and poor transport links, and unemployment.

Trade corridors are formed as a result of trade agreements. In Latin America we find the Central American highway, the Quito-Guayaquil corridor, the

Pan-American Highway in the Andean region, the Buenos Aires-Mendoza-Santiago-Valparaiso corridor, and Brazilian coastal corridors with maritime connections to Asian and European destinations. The development of trade corridors has political, economic, social and environmental implications. Their resilience to the impact of natural hazards is particularly relevant to enhance the sustainable development of cities and regions.

TRENDS IN SOCIO-ECONOMIC VULNERABILITY

The relation of disaster risk and development offers a good starting point to identify macro trends in socio-economic vulnerability. To some degree, socio-economic and environmental vulnerability is shaped by development processes and vice versa. Understanding how patterns of social change and development set the scene for future disasters become crucial to improving disaster risk assessment and analysis, and therefore essential for disaster risk reduction as a whole.

Development and Vulnerability

The analysis of disaster impact shows that an estimated 97 percent of natural disaster related deaths each year occur in developing countries Although smaller in absolute figures, the percentage of economic loss in relation to the GNP in developing countries far exceeds those in developed countries. This fact becomes even more relevant for SIDS. Between 1985 and 1999, the world's wealthiest countries sustained 57.3 percent of the measured economic losses to disasters, representing 2.5 percent of their combined GDP. During the same years, the world's poorest countries endured 24.4 percent of the economic toll of disasters, representing 13.4 percent of their combined GDP.

Some of the vulnerability factors or processes are closely associated with certain types of development models and initiatives. The links between disaster and development are explored in detail in the World Vulnerability Report, currently being developed by UNDP. Increasing or permanent levels of poverty remain as a relevant issue for the analysis of vulnerability trends.

In Southern Africa, poverty levels remain high, especially among the rural poor, with 63.7 percent, 36 percent and 37 per cent of Zambians, Zimbabweans and Mozambicans respectively, living on less than US$ 1 per-day. Their GDP falls far short of per capita GDP in developing countries. Moreover, GDPs for Zambia and Mozambique are around half of those for sub-Saharan Africa. In addition, high levels of foreign debt have discouraged investment and growth, with Zambia shouldering external debts that constitute 181 per cent of its GNP. Under these conditions, it is unrealistic to expect significant investments at household or national level to mitigate the impact of natural or other threats.

Impact of Globalisation

Globalisation has a number of distinctive characteristics that have had a profound influence on the structure of international socioeconomic relations. The impact of globalisation on patterns of vulnerability is critical to identify new trends in disaster risk. The economic dimensions of globalisation include the dominance of a global market, as one of its main features. The combined impacts of economic adjustment measures to encourage greater efficiencies and global competitiveness have been reflected in significant job losses and unemployment. In South Africa alone, between 1996-2000 more than 500,000 formal sector jobs were lost. Between 1997-2000 more than 140,000 miners became unemployed and 50,000 primarily female workers lost their jobs in textile industries. This is an increasingly relevant area which will require further analysis and focus.

Traditional Knowledge at Risk

The pace of technological change and the cultural implications of globalisation pose a real threat to the wealth of local knowledge, and related skills and resources, preserved among indigenous people and in many rural communities.

Economic vulnerability is increasing as local livelihoods are transformed from relying on traditional forms of production to using more intensive or modern methods of agriculture and land use systems. The identification of hazards usually constitutes the departing point for the risk assessment process.

Both hazard and vulnerability/capacity assessments utilise formal procedures that include collection of primary data, monitoring, data processing, mapping, and social surveys techniques, among others. In the case of hazard assessment, where usually high technological developments for monitoring and storing data of geological and atmospheric processes are involved, the assessment activities are mostly restricted to a scientific community. On the other hand, vulnerability and capacity assessments make use of more conventional methodologies and techniques, by which the community at risk may also play an active role, such as in community-based mapping.

Beyond these particularities, hazard and vulnerability/ capacity assessment follow a set of more or less formal procedures that are generally captured under the concept of risk analysis. Seen as this, risk analysis constitutes a core stage of the whole risk assessment process by means of providing relatively objective and technical information from which levels of risk can be estimated.

The information produced by technical risk analysis allows for the establishment of impartial government policy, resources needed for disaster preparedness, and insurance schemes. But from the estimated levels of risk to the determination of acceptable levels of risk, a different range of value judgements are usually taken into account. Socio-economic cost/benefit analyses usually lead to the establishment of priorities that in turn help to draw levels of acceptable risk. These levels will depend largely on government, community priorities, interests and capacities. It is at this stage, particularly, when the more subjective trade-offs of quantitative and qualitative approaches to risk assessment need to be sorted out.

The distinction between risk assessment and risk perception has important implications for disaster risk reduction. In some cases, as in vulnerability/capacity assessment exercises, risk perception may be formally included in the assessment process, by incorporating people's own ideas and perceptions on the risks they are exposed to. Nevertheless, the wide and increasing use of computer assisted techniques and methodologies – such as those involved in Geographic Information Systems (GIS) – may widen the breach between the information produced by technical risk assessments and the understaning of risk by people. Therefore, acceptable levels of risk may vary according to the relative contribution of views on objective risk versus perceived risk, at the various individual, community and institutional scales.

HAZARD ASSESSMENT

The objective of a hazard assessment is to identify the probability of occurrence of a specified hazard, in a specified future time period, as well as its intensity and area of impact. For example, the assessment of flood hazard is extremely important in the design and setting of engineering facilities and in zoning for land use planning. Construction of buildings and residences is often restricted in high flood hazard areas. Flood assessment should be developed for the design and setting of sewage treatment as well as land and buildings having industrial materials of a toxic or dangerous nature, due to the potential spread of contaminants.

Certain hazards have well-established techniques available for their assessment. This is the case for floods, earthquakes and volcanic hazards. Many of the analytical techniques useful for hazard assessment can be applied using medium powered computers and widely available software packages.

On seismic hazards, the dynamic ground shaking and ground movement are the two most important effects considered in the analysis. Dynamic ground shaking is a critical consideration for buildings and construction. The objective of a statistical earthquake hazard assessment is to assess the probability that a particular level of ground motion at a site is reached or exceeded during a specified time interval. An alternative approach is to consider the evaluation of the ground motion produced by the maximum conceivable earthquake in the most unfavourable distance to a specific site. Earthquake hazard assessment in areas of low seismic activity is much more subject to large errors than in areas with high earthquake activity. This is especially the case if the time span of the available data is considerably smaller than the mean return interval of large events, for which the hazard has to be calculated.

In most cases, one is able to characterise the overall activity of a volcano and its potential danger from field observations by mapping the various historical and prehistoric volcanic deposits. These deposits can, in turn, be interpreted in terms of eruptive phenomena, usually by analogy with visually observed eruptions.

Other hazards have less well-defined assessment methodologies. In the future, efforts must continue to increase our understanding and develop methodologies for the assessment of hazards such as heat waves and dust storms; in particular, with regard to the factors which influence their development, movement and decay.

Multi-hazard assessments are difficult to achieve due in part to the different approaches taken by the various disciplines in assessing the specific potential hazards. But multi-hazard assessments are essential, for example, in the case of a tropical storm event. The event cannot be looked at in isolation and should consider the different components that actually represent the risks occurring either separately or all together. These components are flood, landslide, storm surge, tornado and wind. Various hazards will be measured according to different scales, which make comparisons difficult. An earthquake will be quantified based on the amount of energy released (Richter scale) or the amount of damage potentially caused (Modified Mercalli scale), while a heat wave is measured using maximum temperatures and a wind storm using wind velocity.

Vulnerability and Capacity Assessment

Vulnerability and capacity assessments are an indispensable complement to hazard assessment exercises. Despite the considerable efforts and achievements reflected in improved quality and coverage of scientific data on different hazards, the mapping and assessing of social, economic and environmental vulnerabilities of the population are not equally developed. Some aspects of vulnerability/capacity, especially those related to the social nature of these concepts, pose a different range of challenges to risk assessment.

A great deal of work has been focused on the assessment of the physical aspects of vulnerability. This has been done mainly in relation to more conventional hazardous phenomenon, such as windstorms, earthquakes and floods. A high percentage of the vulnerability mapping developments at an earlier stage is reflecting this trend. This was accentuated by the wide utilisation of GIS techniques for the spatial integration of different variables in the 1980s. The spatial overlapping of hazard zones with infrastructure such as airports, main highways, health facilities and power lines, amongst others, is one of the common exercises, highly focused on in the examination of the physical aspects of vulnerability.

The Organisation of American States (OAS) has been one of the pioneers in Latin America in using GIS tools for physical vulnerability assessment, focused on infrastructure and critical facilities. A pilot project launched early in the 1980s on GIS Applications for Natural Hazards Management in Latin America and the Caribbean, implemented more than 200 applications in 20 countries of the region, integrating hazards, natural resources, population and infrastructure data. The fact that it was discovered that all of the main airports in Guatemala are located within high intensity seismic areas, or that 670 kilometres of paved routes in Ecuador were located within a 30 kilometre radius of active volcanos, have been instructive, to say the least.

Several initiatives towards comprehensive risk assessments are currently going on in the Pacific islands states. In the Cook Islands, for example, risk assessments related to tropical cyclones and associated flooding have been undertaken. These include both the technical aspects of hazard mapping, vulnerability assessments of building stock, infrastructure, lifelines and critical facilities, and the social aspects of potential economic losses and impacts on communities. The risk assessment information provided input for community early warning systems for tropical cyclones, ERWIN, as well as primary information for reports and technical support materials such as: Cook Islands Building Code; Disaster Management Work Plan; National Disaster Management Plan; Cyclone Response Procedures; Tsunami Response Procedures.

.nother good example for this region is provided by Fiji, where in recent years, several comprehensive risk assessment projects have been undertaken. These have always involved the relevant government departments and infrastructure agencies, and include representation from NGOs and the private sector. The participation of international agencies and/or consultants which has ensured that up-to-date methodologies and technologies were employed.

Methodological challenges

While hazard mapping and physical aspects of vulnerability analysis have been substantially facilitated and improved due to the use of GIS techniques, the inclusion of social, economic and environmental variables into GIS's conceptual models, remains as a major methodological challenge. The need to assign a quantifiable value to the variables analysed into the spatial models used by GIS is not always possible for some social/economic dimensions of vulnerability – for instance, how to quantify the ideological and cultural aspects of vulnerability. Moreover, the diverse scales – individual, family, community, regional – at which different dimensions of socio-economic vulnerability operate, makes the spatial representation through these techniques, very difficult.

The quality and detail of the information required by the analysis facilitated by GIS is, in many cases, inexistent, especially in LDCs and other developing countries. In general, the quality and availability of statistical data sets limit the information for GIS analysis to low resolution outputs. The use of GIS for vulnerability/ capacity analysis is still at an embryonic stage, in comparison with its wide use in hazard mapping. Several research initiatives are aiming to bring solutions to the current methodological constraints, especially the quantification of social aspects of vulnerability. Still, the socio-economic vulnerability assessments rely on more conventional ways, which indeed provide other opportunities and advantages, such as the active involvement of the community at risk in exercises as community based mapping and assessments.

7

Institutional Frameworks for Disaster Management

Disaster risk management needs to be motivated and based within governmental responsibilities, but its success cannot be accomplished without the benefits of widespread decision-making and the participation of many others. Leading policy direction is crucial and legal foundations assure a continuing legitimacy, but it is the professional and human resources delivered on the ground that are a measure of success. For this to happen, there must be a systematic approach to relate local decision-making processes with larger administrative and resource capabilities such as those devised in provincial or state and national disaster plans and risk reduction strategies.

EMERGING INSTITUTIONAL FRAMEWORKS FOR DISASTER REDUCTION

International Decade for Natural Disaster Reduction (IDNDR) programme not only provided an institutional framework for countries, but also introduced basic concepts of disaster reduction to administrators and professionals. It started the task of shifting policy emphasis from post-disaster relief and rebuilding to a more proactive approach of disaster preparedness and mitigation.

For a long time, the state was considered the centre of all authority as well as action in dealing with disasters. Communities were considered generally unaware of the hazards they faced. As a result, disaster management was most often understood as providing relief to victims, aiding recovery following an event, and rebuilding damaged infrastructure. As people tended not to thirık so much about disaster reduction strategies beforehand or how to reduce risk to disasters, politicians and official authorities have tended to rely heavily upon emergency assistance whenever the need arose. These outlooks also have been perpetuated by the extent of international funds and local emergency allocations that easily become available after a disaster rather than before.

Historically there have been many fewer resources devoted to routine hazard identification and assessment activities or to support sustained risk management strategies in areas of known and recurrent natural disaster risks. This may result from an institutional lack of appreciation for public safety and the economic values of prevention in contrast to the cost of replacing lost assets. Alternaiely, it may reflect the persistent difficulty in demonstrating costefficiencies involved in saving lives and public property from disasters before they occur.

While disaster management and response coordination can benefit from centralised command there is a need to decentralise disaster risk reduction. Along with the decentralisation of power and devolution of governing authority, disaster risk reduction at the local community level needs to be encouraged, and supported. The decentralisation of responsibility for disaster risk reduction has to be coordinated by municipalities, townships, wards or local communities. Mutual understanding and rules and regulations should be explicit, transparent and uniform. This requires a new structural arrangement in which national authorities of countries, UN agencies, bilateral development agencies and financial institutions implement projects in risk reduction not only with national governments but also with local authorities, the private sector, academic institutions, community-based organisations and NGOs.

However, there are currently few local institutions ready to fill the vacuum to assist communities in owning and internalising the process of risk reduction, in terms of concept, knowledge, and implementation. Almost all countries or local communities have a designated authority responsible for responding to crisis situations when they happen; many fewer have a recognised office or agency charged with monitoring potential risks to the society and motivating concerted public and private action to minimise their potential consequences.

Such a change in the emphasis of governmental functions requires that a consensus be developed on the respective roles of government agencies, commercial interests, communities and individuals themselves. Governments have vital roles to play in disaster risk management that must vary according to each of their respective needs and conditions, but there is now widespread recognition that they must focus their limited resources and serve as co-ordinating bodies if they are to become more effective.

Institutional Disaster Frameworks Management in Asian Countries

Disaster risk management is a concept that is interpreted differently in various Asian countries. There is a wide variation among the primary ministries or national agencies designated to assume disaster management responsibilities in different countries. This reflects either the predominant types of hazards which threaten individual countries, or else stems from an historical outlook of what has commonly constituted disaster management responsibilities. Until a recent change taking place in 2002, for almost 50 years the Central National Authority for disaster management in India had been located within the Ministry of Agriculture, reflecting that country's historical concerns with flood, drought or famine. As elsewhere, until recently, most government institutions tended to concentrate on the emergency services associated with post-disaster rescue, relief, reconstruction and rehabilitation, as well as maintaining public law and order during times of crisis.

Concepts of risk management have begun to take hold in some Asian countries at national levels. Thailand is poised to revamp its disaster management system and plans to set up a new department of disaster management in the Ministry of Interior from October 2002. Both Laos and Cambodia have established or re-configured their respective national disaster management offices with encouragement and support from UNDP and other international organisations. The Philippines is considering new legislation to widen the scope of its existing Office of Civil Defence and the National Disaster Coordinating Council.

Viet Nam has undertaken a major sustained effort to formulate a 20 year strategic plan for disaster risk management. This effort has been steered largely by in-country expertise and was reviewed in an international consultation held in March 2002. Following the establishment of its Disaster Management Bureau in the renamed Ministry of Disaster Management and Relief in 1992, the government of Bangladesh is proceeding to develop and progressively implement a comprehensive disaster management programme during 2000-2002. Increasingly, more Asian countries are also including some reference to disaster risk reduction in their national development plans. Over the last decade, UNDP has supported capacity building projects for disaster risk management in over ten Asian countries.

Two additional examples can be cited from countries in Asia, which together account for almost a third of the world's population: India and China. These countries share many of the same types of hazards spread over vast land areas and have adopted approaches for centuries that have taken risk into account in a variety of technical endeavours. While both countries are populated by people with many different cultural outlooks, each of them has different structures of government. Tellingly, they have each demonstrated renewed commitments in recent years to reorient their national strategies of disaster management to take greater account of the benefits to be derived from disaster risk reduction.

As the Indian sub-continent is highly vulnerable to natural and related disasters, with losses mounting every year, government authorities in India have recognised the pressing importance of developing more effective disaster management policies. At the operational level, there have been equal concerns to strengthen related organisational arrangements that can lessen the widespread impacts of disasters such as by updating state codes, manuals and disaster plans on the basis of experience gained and taking account of technological developments. Initiatives have been taken to conduct comprehensive revisions of disaster policies giving greater attention to reducing risk factors in the state of Maharashtra following the devastation of the Latur earthquake in 1997 and in the state of Uttar Pradesh in 1999. The creation of the new state of Uttarakhand has provided the opportunity to reconsider the most appropriate forms of disaster management structures for its mountainous topography. The rapid and severe repercussions of the more recent destruction resulting from the 1999 cyclone in the state of

Orissa, and then the Bhuj earthquake in 2001 in the state of Gujarat have spurred a similarly intensified commitment to alter the long-standing standing relief commissioner system and to revise national policies of risk reduction. A High Powered Committee on Disaster Management Plans (HPC-DMP) has been constituted with the approval of the Prime Minister to:

- Review existing arrangements for preparedness and mitigation of natural and human induced disasters including industrial, nuclear, biological and chemical disasters.
- Recommend measures for strengthening organisational structures.
- Recommend a comprehensive model for disaster management at national, state and district levels.

In proceeding beyond its original mandate confined only to the preparation of plans for natural disasters, the HPC-DMP recommended that the human dimension of disasters also needed to be included in adopting a more holistic approach to disaster management planning. As a result, additional considerations will be extended to include forecasting and warning systems, public awareness, proactive measures to reduce risk in development programmes, development of human resources, information technology, networking and coordinating organisational relationships, and updating building codes and practices.

A National Centre for Disaster Management has been engaged to undertake human resource development studies, to develop a database and to provide documentation in the area of natural disaster mitigation and preparedness. These institutional developments and expanded outlooks go well beyond the more immediately obvious concerns first associated with the need for updated emergency control rooms and improved response mechanisms that will also be considered in the comprehensive review.

The HPC-DMP has demonstrated a highlevel government commitment in forming a National Committee on Disaster Management constituted under the chairmanship of the prime minister and comprising the heads of all the national and provincial political parties. The committee, which also includes technical specialists, respected academicians and key civil servants, has been tasked to suggest short, medium and long-term steps for strengthening relief and rehabilitation capabilities and to identify measures that can reduce natural calamities in the future.

The work programme is striving to involve an expanded range of professional interests ranging from the responsibilities of local government, revenue allocation and insurance, through the practice of engineering, public works, education and public administration. More than 30 different hazards have been identified by the HPCDMP, and nodal ministries have been engaged to work on national plans for the potential disaster risks related to water and climate, geology, industrial and nuclear activities, transportation accidents and biological threats. Even though the HPC-DMP's mandate is to produce plans, it has embarked on an inclusive planning process that emphasises the participation of all relevant organisations and sectors. This systematic approach devolves disaster management planning activities from strictly a national concern to one involving state, district and local officials.

A decision was taken by the Indian government in early 2002 to alter almost 50 years of practice by relocating all matters regarding disaster and risk management to the Ministry of Home Affairs. This reflects a departure from the previous association of natural disasters with the predominant concerns of food supplies and agriculture and signals a promising opportunity to engage many additional functional responsibilities and authoritative aspects of government. As the influential Ministry of Home Affairs is directly responsible for the coordination and management of the operational aspects of government, and its influence proceeds from national direction of the civil service all the way down to local levels of implementation of government policies, this is an important step to integrate disaster risk management issues more fully into many more national planning processes.

China presents another approach yet also displays similar emphasis. During the course of the IDNDR, the Chinese government recognised that working for disaster reduction would require a long-term commitment and it has worked with dedication and political commitment at the highest levels of responsibility to fulfil those objectives by actively responding to the direction of UN/ISDR. The Chinese government established the Chinese National Committee for International Disaster Reduction (CNCIDR) in October 2000 consisting of 30 official agencies, including the State Council, ministries, national committees and bureaus, the military services and additional social groups. CNCIDR is an inter-ministerial coordinating institution led by a State Councillor responsible for designing a national disaster reduction framework, developing guiding policies, coordinating relevant departments in the conduct of specific programmes, and supervising disaster reduction works undertaken by local governments. An additional advisory group of 28 senior experts in relevant fields has been formed to provide guidance to the national committee especially on applying science and technology in realising disaster reduction initiatives. The office of CNCIDR and its secretariat are located in the Ministry of Civil Affairs.

By embracing the importance of disaster reduction activities, China has proceeded to integrate the subject into overall national economic and social development planning. The core element of this process is the progressive implementation of the National Disaster Reduction Plan of the People's Republic of China (NDRP) running from 1998 to 2010. The NDRP was launched by the Chinese government in April 1998, and significantly, it was formulated on the basis of the overall national development policies reflected in the "Ninth Five Year Plan for National Economic and Social Development", and the "2010 Prospective Target Outline" for national accomplishments. The formulation of the plan received important support and technical assistance from UNDP, further demonstrating the essential links between disaster risk reduction and national development interests.

The NDRP was based on several fundamental policies that demonstrate both the breadth and the depth of interests that have been marshalled to develop and implement a national strategy for disaster reduction. The primary orientation of the strategy of disaster reduction is to serve the advancement of national economic and social development. In this respect, a principle has been formulated to assign the top priority to disaster reduction activities, while also recognising that there will still be the requirement to combine these with disaster response and emergency relief efforts at the time of crisis. A focus is to be placed on key elements of disaster reduction work, while keeping a view throughout on the long-term strategic objectives of disaster reduction.

The roles of science, technology and education are considered to be of particular importance in building disaster reduction into a national concept. To succeed, it will be essential to encourage the involvement of all elements from the national and local governments and the fullest possible participation from all the professions and trades, working together. It will also remain important for China to be closely involved with international developments in disaster reduction and therefore must strive to strengthen its own efforts of international exchanges and multinational cooperation in the field.

Objectives outlined by the NDRP include efforts to:

— Develop a set of projects which are of importance to advancing the social and economic development in China.

— Increase the application of scientific and technical experience and the benefits of new achievements in disaster reduction work.

— Enhance public awareness and knowledge about disaster reduction.

— Establish comprehensive organisational abilities and operational structures for realising specific activities in disaster risk reduction.

— Reduce the impact of natural disasters on national economy and social development, as measured by an obvious reduction in the direct economic losses caused by natural disasters.

The NDRP has also outlined specific tasks, measures and key activities that should be pursued nationwide. In this respect, one of the most important works for CNCIDR is to implement the plan first at provincial levels, and then also at local levels of responsibility. Several provinces have issued mid-term plans on disaster reduction in their specific areas, as can be seen in the Provinces of Guangdong, Jiangxi, Yunnan, and Shanxi. In others, such as in Heilongjiang, the national government is working closely with the provincial authorities to initiate a local programme strategy.

In order to further the implementation of the NDRP, the CNCIDR is organising a number of meetings at senior levels to share experiences among the provinces and to discuss the guidelines on forming local disaster reduction plans with officials drawn from different sectors. China's response to the ISDR secretariat questionnaire in 2001 also cited that one of the most important issues to be addressed was to improve capacity building, especially in terms of early warning systems, the development of resilient infrastructure and the application of technologies to form a safer society.

In many Asian countries, however, a lack of uniformity in policy approaches remains regarding the various aspects of disaster management allocated among different ministries. This also poses additional hindrances for improving regional or sub-regional cooperation. It is unlikely that the Home Ministry of Nepal, the national focal point, could have developed the degree of interaction and understanding desired with its comparable national disaster focal point in India, previously located in the Ministry of Agriculture.

The prominent involvement of the water authorities, and the additional policy concerns of the Ministry of Disaster Management and Relief in Bangladesh further complicate the potential for effective relationships in such matters. This would be useful since the cause and progress of floods can easily affect all three countries. Furthermore, all three countries have additional ministries and related technical agencies concerned with water resources as well as environmental affairs. This represents a serious and growing impediment as one accepts that many natural hazards and disaster conditions affect more than one country, or involve the skills and technical abilities of many professions.

These conditions underlines the challenges posed when decisions taken in one location can easily impact the scale of consequences in neighbouring countries, or even among different socio-economic segments of the population in the countries. More informed and considered efforts are required to bring these various professional specialists and civil authorities together, other than just through occasional international meetings, if a coherent disaster risk management strategy with local public relevance is to be realised in practice.

Institutional Disaster Frameworks Management in in America

A major shift is now taking place in many countries in the Americas, from the north to the south. The combination of extremely severe social, economic and environmental consequences associated with several disasters in the final years of the 1990s provided stark and unavoidable lessons to leaders in the region.

Both official and public outlooks about disasters in Latin America and the Caribbean countries prior to 1990 concentrated almost exclusively on developing humanitarian response and improving preparedness capacities, linked to civil defence or military institutions.

The 1990s would see some important institutional changes in emphasis and priorities, starting already in 1985 in Mexico and Colombia after a major earthquake and volcanic eruption respectively. Disaster reduction issues, expressed through terms of prevention and mitigation and given a higher status in political and technical discourse, although this was not transferred into significant changes or real action during much of the decade. Most official disaster organisations created prevention offices in name, but their roles were limited essentially to strengthening efforts in disaster preparedness, conducting basic hazard mapping or promoting early warning systems at national scales. Few human or financial resources were committed and existing legal and institutional arrangements impeded any major changes.

Linking risk reduction with development policies and environmental concerns is common in several Central American countries, especially where the severe effects of hurricane Mitch decimated earlier investments made in national development. In 1996, Guatemala reformed its disaster legislation and created the National Coordinator for Disaster Reduction (CONRED) comprising a supervisory council of representatives from different development departments, disaster response agencies, and civil society. While serving neither as a single organisation nor a system, CONRED was given an expanded range of responsibilities in the field of risk reduction, and has provided a focal point for expanded attention to risk issues. By working together with the Ministry of Planning, a National Risk Reduction System is being established and efforts are underway to incorporate multi-sector risk reduction strategies into the country's National Poverty Reduction Plan. These activities complement the longstanding Disaster Response Division and an Emergency Operations Centre.

In recent years, aided by UNDP, Nicaragua has developed an expanded approach for a National Programme for Risk Reduction and has designed a new disaster risk management strategy. First, studies were commissioned to analyse the Nicaraguan legal framework for disaster management and the implications regarding government, municipalities, the private sector and citizens. Early in 2000, the Nicaraguan National Legislative Assembly passed a new law creating the National System for Disaster Prevention, Mitigation and Attention and officially established the National Risk Reduction Plan as a central operational instrument. As seen elsewhere, the institutional concept was built upon a broad and comprehensive approach to risk reduction issues, but one that is intended to be implemented on a decentralised basis. The strategy and the legislation are considered by some commentators to be the most advanced examples for disaster reduction in the region at the present time. Both Swiss bilateral development assistance and World Bank support have been enlisted to strengthen the provision of technical abilities and to augment human resources. While the implementation of the process can benefit by drawing on the combined experiences of the Civil Defence Organisation and the Nicaraguan Institute for Territorial Studies, the key to future success will be the extent to which productive relationships can be forged with other key government departments and development agencies.

In part spurred on by the social and economic consequences of a particularly severe ice storm in 2000, the Canadian Prime Minister announced the creation of the Office of Critical Infrastructure Protection and Emergency Preparedness (OCIPEP) in February 2001. The office was established to enhance the protection of Canada's critical infrastructure from disruption or destruction, and to act as the government of Canada's primary agency for ensuring national civil emergency preparedness. Critical infrastructure (which includes energy and utilities, communications, services, transportation, safety and government) constitutes the backbone of the nation's economy, and is essential to the health, security, safety and economic wellbeing of all Canadians and to the effective functioning of government.

The Minister of National Defence is responsible for this organisation, which encompasses all the responsibilities of the previously named Emergency Preparedness Canada (EPC). With a necessarily broader mandate than the EPC, OCIPEP takes an all-hazards approach, recognising that different hazardous events can have similar impacts. The office provides national leadership to help ensure the protection of infrastructure, in both its physical and cyber dimensions, regardless of the source of the threat. This includes developing and promoting activities which reduce vulnerabilities against various threats and thus mitigate the impacts of disasters.

OCIPEP seeks to enhance the capacity of individuals, communities, businesses and governments in Canada to effectively manage risks to their physical and cyber environments. Although OCIPEP is a new organisation, its responsibilities relating to civil emergency preparedness and planning have a long history. Through the former EPC, a great deal of experience in preparedness, response and recovery activities have been gained, resulting in Canada's increasingly comprehensive ability to cope with emergency situations. Mitigation, while an important part of disaster management, has largely been an implicit requirement. There have always been efforts across the nation to mitigate disasters, including land use zoning guidelines and structural protective features such as the Red River Floodway in Manitoba. These mitigating actions have a common thread: they reduce the probability of a calamity or limit the effect of a disaster should it happen.

However, it had been recognised by various groups and individuals, that there existed a need to address hazard mitigation in Canada in a more explicit and systematic way. A National Mitigation Workshop was hosted by EPC and the Insurance Bureau of Canada in 1998, attended by academic, private sector and government representatives. It concluded that a comprehensive national mitigation initiative would be a positive step towards the long term goal of reducing vulnerabilities to, and losses from, disasters. These ideals have been reinforced by participants of the ongoing

Canadian Natural Hazards Assessment Project (CNHAP) in which a community of scientists, scholars and practitioners in the natural hazards and disasters field came together early in 2000 to begin a major new examination of the national understanding about the causes and consequences of natural hazards and disasters.

In light of a number of multidisciplinary discussions regarding emergency management and disaster reduction, the Government of Canada announced in June 2001 that OCIPEP will lead consultations on the development of a National Disaster Mitigation Strategy (NDMS). These consultations will include all levels of government, private sector and non-governmental stakeholders, in order to solicit their input and participation in defining the framework for this new national strategy. This important step is being taken in the recognition that new measures should be developed "to save lives, reduce the impact of disasters and the resulting damages and costs to the Canadian public".

As a part of this process OCIPEP intends to issue a discussion paper to help stimulate discussions regarding the NDMS, in the hopes of obtaining views from various stakeholders on the possible scope, policies and mechanisms for coordinating and implementing a national strategy. Meanwhile, the federal government continues to conduct inter-departmental discussions about federal mitigation activities, through an Interdepartmental Mitigation Coordinating Committee. Participants include representatives from all relevant federal departments who are reviewing preparedness and mitigation initiatives and conducting analysis to identify areas where additional attention is needed.

The National Plan for the Prevention of Disasters, promulgated in Colombia in 1998, gave little attention to anticipatory measures or specific risk reduction practices during non-crisis situations. More recently, however, the National Council for Social and Economic Policy has incorporated disaster reduction measures explicitly into the individual sectoral plans of the National Development Plan. Accordingly, in 2001, the National Council for Social and Economic Policy developed a strategy to initiate the short-term and medium-term execution of the National Disaster Prevention and Management Plan.

The strategy is an example of a comprehensive initiative to improve the National Plan for the Prevention of Disasters. It "outlines the work to be advanced for the following three years and establishes the first steps for the consolidation of the National Plan in the medium-term. It identifies the objectives of action and the responsible individuals, expediting the National Plan's work in mitigating natural disasters and their levels of risk in Colombia. Additionally, this national effort seeks to meet the goals of the UN-ISDR and to comply with the initiatives of the Meeting of the Americas in the framework of the Andean Community."

The National Council for Social and Economic Policy has cited four accomplishments that have to be met if its strategy is to be implemented successfully:

- Strengthen public awareness campaigns on natural disasters.
- Initiate regional and sectoral planning for disaster prevention.
- Institutionalise the national disaster prevention and management plan.
- Communicate the national plan to the public and to the authorities.

This updated and revitalised strategy was approved by the President of Colombia as well as by the country's National Planning Department and all the relevant ministries of interior, economic development, finance and public credit, agriculture and rural development, education, health, environment, energy, communications, transportation, labour and social security, culture and national defence. Most importantly, this strategy is linked to budgetary allocations within the respective institutions.

One example of the strategy's implementation in practice can be seen in the city of Manizales where a local environmental action plan has been established through widespread consultation with the community. The plan is integrated into the municipality's development plan and budget, and includes specific measures to reduce the risk of landslides and seeks to relocate the population living on steep slopes. These programmes are also linked to the development of ecological parks some of which are located on slopes too dangerous for settlements, and others have been integrated into the city's watershed thereby protecting their important economic functions.

In Bolivia too, a comprehensive national policy for prevention and risk management has been established recently. Consistent with the intentions of the Andean Regional Programme for Risk Prevention and Reduction (PREANDINO), the Minister of Sustainable Development and Planning has announced the government's commitment to formulate policies and strategies for the incorporation of disaster prevention in the planning system through the National Plan for Prevention and Risk Mitigation. It is anticipated that mechanisms will be established with necessary legislation in order to introduce elements of prevention with the various sectoral initiatives. In this regard, the work of prevention may be considered as complementary to the objectives of sustainable development.

The government has recently been pressing ahead with several national programmes aimed at incorporating prevention into the management of development activities, such as the Programme for Risk Prevention and Reduction financed by UNDP and the World Bank. Another programme financed by the German Agency for Technical Cooperation (GTZ) the Local Risk Management Programme. In housing, the National Housing Subsidy Programme, financed by employer contributions, includes a Prevention and Risk Mitigation Sub-Programme. The Ministry of Agriculture, livestock livestock and rural development is implementing a National Food Security Monitoring and Early Warning System, which will be responsible for monitoring the impact of natural disasters on agricultural production. UNESCO, working jointly with this ministry, is also progressing in its support for a programme linking developmental issues and the risk issues associated with the El Niño phenomenon.

Risk management has also been introduced in a guide to adapting municipal development plans, which is to be implemented in 30 pilot municipalities. These will ensure that municipal plans for risk prevention and mitigation will be in line with national and sectoral policies. Manuals are being prepared on how to draw up municipal plans for risk prevention and mitigation in relation to town and country planning, human settlements and environmental management.

Institutional Disaster Frameworks Management in African Countries

A methodical, if protracted, effort to develop a comprehensive national strategy for disaster risk management has been pursued in South Africa by reforming organisational structures and creating new legislation concerning disaster risk management. As so often happens, it was after a severe crisis – flooding in the Cape Flats in 1994 – that the government resolved to assess South Africa's ability to deal with disaster risk management. This initially involved a complete review of disaster management structures and policies. A year later, the cabinet recommended that a formal structure for disaster management be established. An initial National Disaster Management Committee was formed in 1996 with the intended function of coordinating and managing national disaster management policy. As that body never came into its own right, by mid-1997 the government approved the formation of an alternate Inter-Ministerial Committee for Disaster Management (IMC).

At this stage, a decision was taken to produce a Green Paper on Disaster Management for all levels of government (national, provincial and local) as the first tangible step to establish a formal disaster management policy for the country. It was tabled in February 1998 with the aim to ensure that a comprehensive disaster management system could be realised and implemented by means of a national strategy that would be more fully elaborated in a subsequent policy White Paper on Disaster Management. The Green Paper provided an important conceptual framework for disaster management and risk reduction. A year later in January 1999, the White Paper was able to build on these views by emphasising the risk and disaster reduction issues highlighted by the international and regional trends at the time. The White Paper was developed within the framework of the IDNDR, and importance also was given to developing joint standards and common practices among the other 13 countries of the Southern African Development Community (SADC).

Key policy proposals contained in the White Paper included:

— Integration of risk reduction strategies into development initiatives.

— Development of a strategy to reduce the most vulnerable communities.

— Legal establishment of a National Disaster Management Centre (authority).

— Introduction of a new disaster management funding strategy.

— Introduction and implementation of a new Disaster Management Act.

— Establishment of a framework to enable communities to be informed, alert and self-reliant and be capable of supporting and cooperating with government in disaster reduction activities.

— Establishment of a framework to coordinate training and community awareness initiatives.

Meanwhile, in order to address South Africa's immediate needs, an interim disaster management authority was composed with representatives from ten national departments. This was later converted into a National Disaster Management Centre (NDMC). However, despite the fact that it has been operational since 1999, it has yet to become a statutory institution. An Inter-Departmental Disaster Management Committee (IDMC) was also established in the same year to ensure better coordination among government departments at national level. This, however, was intended as an interim measure until such time when the planned statutory structures contained in a Disaster Management Bill could become functional under a new Disaster Management Act.

Following the issuance of the White Paper, the first Disaster Management Bill was published for public comment in 2000. However, the initial enthusiasm and momentum shown by the government seemed to decline with numerous postponements of the tabling of the bill. After another severe crisis – this time, the devastating floods in parts of Southern Africa in 2000 political priorities changed as the importance of disaster management policy and legislation resurfaced. The National Council of Provinces called for a disaster management conference in May 2000 to consider disaster management and reduction on a regional basis. After this conference, encouraged by funding from a bilateral disaster assistance agency, the South African legislative process regained momentum and the bill was finally tabled for debate, with approval anticipated during the latter part of 2002.

During its lengthy review, the Disaster Management Bill has moved away somewhat from the earlier policy emphasis envisioned in the Green and White Papers and instead has focussed more attention on inter-governmental structures and related operational frameworks. The bill provides guidance with respect to the legal establishment of the NDMC, the duties and powers of national, provincial and local instruments of government and funding for post-disaster recovery and rehabilitation. The rationale behind the robustness of the bill is to ensure that clear and unambiguous guidelines can be given through regulations once the legislation is promulgated. The bill also provides for an Inter-governmental Committee on Disaster Management to consist of cabinet members involved in disaster management, members of the Executive Councils from the nine provinces of the country and representatives of local government. A further structure proposed in the bill is the National Disaster Management Framework, which will outline coherent, transparent and inclusive policies on all aspects of disaster management including training and capacity building.

Expected to become law during 2002, the Bill calls for the establishment of disaster management centres at all levels of government, and also establishes procedures for the collection and dissemination of risk assessment data and information. One of the explicit functions of the centres will be the assessment of disaster risks, with the requirement that each one also serve as a repository and conduit for information relating to all aspects of disasters, impending disasters and disaster management. The overall thrust is one that can develop a national disaster management framework that would reflect a balanced consideration of the different kinds of disasters, and the varying severity or magnitudes that occur in southern Africa. Emphasis has also been given to measures that could reduce the vulnerability of disaster-prone areas, communities and households. The anticipated Disaster Management Act is expected to open up new avenues for greater commitment to be made by provincial and local government authorities to undertake risk assessment activities.

The NDMC has been conceived to be responsible not only for pre-disaster activities, risk and vulnerability reduction but also for postdisaster rehabilitation and recovery actions. A predominant part of the methodology underlying the NDMC is the management of actual disaster situations through all aspects of the disaster management cycle. Emphasis is also placed on the important role of the NDMC in the areas of training and community awareness. Consistent with regional trends, the NDMC and the IDMC are to be actively involved in the SADC initiative to establish a regional disaster management coordinating framework.

One of the principal challenges for evolving government institutions in Mozambique has been the recurrent need to respond to emergency conditions. Since its independence in 1975, considerable resources have been channelled into disaster management, and institutions have continually evolved to deal with new and challenging conditions. This hard-won experience has produced a seasoned cadre of disaster managers throughout the government and a well developed inter-ministerial structure for the coordination of disaster management.

It is much to the government's credit that for some time it has recognised the importance of shifting its emphasis in disaster management from immediate response and rehabilitation needs to the long-term values of mitigation and risk reduction. In the last few years, there has been a dedicated effort supported by the highest levels of government to bring together this experience and establish formal structures and procedures that can build capacities for improved disaster risk management in the future.

From as early as 1981, the Government of Mozambique was attentive to the need to address the consequences of risk on the society. A Department for the Prevention and Control of Natural Disasters (DPCCN) was established with the objective of promoting early warning and mitigation activities. During a period of complex national emergency from about 1982 to 1994 DPCCN became a principal conduit for international aid to people displaced by conflict and the victims of repeated floods and droughts, with logistics becoming its predominant activity. With improved conditions and changing needs in the country, a process was begun in 1996 supported by the WFP as DPCCN's principal international partner, to formulate a coherent National Disaster Management Policy and to reorient disaster management towards risk reduction activities.

During the closing years of the 1990s, this involved sustained efforts to reinvent institutions and revise policies created in the prolonged period of permanent emergency, as well as to stimulate an evolution in attitudes, both within government and in the population as a whole. As expressed in current national policies, the primary objective has been to break the vicious cycle of continually expending scarce resources in emergency response and reconstruction, only then to become vulnerable and unprepared for the next catastrophic event.

In 1999, with the approval of the Council of Ministers, the Mozambican government created new institutions to give greater coherence and a clear mandate for government structures dealing with disasters. The Coordinating Counsel for Disaster Management (CCGC) was composed at the ministerial level as the principal government body for coordinating disaster management in all its phases. A National Institute for Disaster Management (INGC) was created to serve as its permanent technical support unit, with the director of INGC chairing an additional multi-sectoral Technical Committee for Disaster Management (CTGC) to assure strong coordination and collaboration in planning, mitigation, and response activities.

A proposed National Law on Disaster Management will serve as a legal mandate for the implementation of policy, with the principal objective stated in the first article, "to avoid the occurrence or minimise the effects of disasters". In particular, it gives the National Disaster Management Plan, as approved by the Council of Ministers, the force of law. While yet to be finalised, the national policy will entail a framework for the coordination of government entities, the participation of civil society and collaboration with the private sector in all aspects of disaster management. In addition, the law will establish sanctions for individuals or organisations violating the provisions of a declared state of emergency.

Under the mandate of the CTGC, a series of studies have been conducted to ensure that national policies are translated into concrete actions and that these norms are codified in the disaster management legislation under consideration. As these proposed objectives require the evaluation of potential hazards as well as their impacts on the local population, the organisations that comprise the CTGC are expected to carry out both historical analysis of disaster vulnerability and risk as well as to conduct assessments of current conditions in an annual process of contingency planning. Unfortunately, the vicious cycle also affects international agencies, from UN organisations to local NGOs. In October 1999, the government of Mozambique released its contingency plan for the up-coming rainy season, noting the high probability of floods in the southern and central regions of the country. At that time it requested international assistance of US$ 2.7 million for immediate preparedness and mitigation activities. The response to this appeal was poor with less than half of the requested funds pledged by the international community. Yet only six months later, in the wake of terrible flooding, the international community gave US$ 100 million in emergency assistance and relief. Subsequently, international pledges for rehabilitation activities following the floods exceeded US$ 450 million.

At the individual level there may also be reason for concern as there is some indication that populations have become dependent on emergency assistance and therefore have a strong incentive to maintain their vulnerability. Given such a disproportionate application of available resources, it is not difficult to see why effective reform may prove difficult to sustain.

8

Disaster Preparedness

Traditionally disaster risks have not been a priority on the development agenda. When carefully laid development plans are tragically interrupted by disasters, the international community relies on organisations such as the United Nations and the Red Cross to step in with relief services. When the emergency work is over, reconstruction efforts are initiated to get the country "back on the development track". Clearly, most poverty reduction programmes leave a lot to be desired in terms of integration with disaster management.

PARADIGM SHIFTS—FROM RELIEF AND RESPONSE TO DISASTER RISK MANAGEMENT

The paradigm shift in poverty reduction programmes—from income poverty to human poverty—has almost been matched in the disaster management sector. Disasters are no longer seen as extreme events, created entirely by natural forces, but as manifestations of unresolved problems of development.

Disaster management practices have evolved from a largely top-down relief and response approach to a more intersectoral risk management approach. In current risk management approaches, there is more room than ever for addressing the issues of risk reduction for the poor.

Till a few decades ago, disasters were viewed as one-off events and responded to by governments and relief agencies without taking into account the social and economic implications and causes of these events. Following our much-improved understanding of the natural processes that underlie hazardous events, a more technocratic paradigm came into existence—"the only way to deal with disasters was by public policy application of geophysical and engineering knowledge". Disasters were regarded as exceptional events, not related to the ongoing social and developmental processes. Gradually this attitude changed to an emphasis on preparedness measures, such as stockpiling of relief goods, preparedness plans and a growing role for relief agencies such as the Red Cross. This "contingency planning" approach certainly improved the efficiency of relief agencies but left a lot to be desired in terms of the appropriateness and effectiveness of relief work.

From the 1960s to the 2008s, there was an exponential increase in human and material losses from disaster events, although there was no clear evidence that the frequency of extreme hazard events had increased. This indicated that the rise in disasters and their consequences was related to a rise in the vulnerability of people all over the world, possibly as a result of development determined by human action. The increase in vulnerability was not uniform, with large variations across regions, nations, provinces, cities, communities, socio-economic classes, castes and even gender. An earthquake of magnitude 6.4 occurred in San Fernando, California in 1971. In a city of over seven million people, only 58 deaths were reported. Two years later, a similar earthquake, registering a magnitude of 6.2 on the Richter scale, in Managua, reduced the center of the city to rubble and killed over 6,000 people. Similar patterns can be seen in other recent disasters.

From the realisation that people's vulnerability is a key factor determining the impact of disasters, emphasis shifted to using "vulnerability analysis" as a tool in disaster management. In recent years, a more comprehensive approach known as disaster risk management, has emerged. This approach has three distinct but interrelated components: hazard assessment, vulnerability analysis and enhancement of management capacity. It is more closely integrated with the ongoing development processes. Disasters are no longer viewed as extreme events created entirely by natural forces but as unresolved problems of development. It is now recognised that risks (physical, social and economic), unmanaged (or mismanaged) for a long time, lead to the occurrence of disasters.

This evolution of approaches, from relief and response to risk management, has begun to influence the way disaster management programmes are now being planned and financed. There are initiatives aimed at reducing social and economic vulnerability and investing in long-term mitigation activities. Unfortunately such initiatives are few, poorly funded and insignificant in comparison with money spent by donors and development banks on humanitarian assistance and relief, as well as on post-disaster reconstruction.

Another weakness is that such initiatives are often taken up in the formal sector of the economy, and bypass the poor and the most vulnerable sections of society. As Maskrey points out, "in the year or so between the occurrence of a disaster and approved national reconstruction plans, many vulnerable communities revert to coping with risk, often in the same or worse conditions than before the disaster actually struck." There is more need than ever to address the issues of risk reduction for the poor. As is the case in mainstream development, there is also a need to focus on good governance, accountability and bottom-up approaches.

New approaches to disaster and poverty reduction have a number of common features:

(i) The approaches developed to be more people-centered.

(ii) The development of a multisectoral approach in planning and decision making.

(iii) The increasing importance of improving access to resources.

(iv) Their contribution to the overall development process In spite of these common elements, the poverty and disaster reduction efforts have developed as parallel processes rather than as integral processes, probably due to a lack of thorough understanding of their linkage and the benefits deriving from this.

POVERTY AND VULNERABILITY

While it is clear that the poor are often those most affected by a disaster, it is too simplistic to assume that there is a direct and absolute correlation between poverty and vulnerability. Poverty, as an indicator of lack of access to resources and income opportunities, is only one of the several dimensions of vulnerability. A poor community may be economically vulnerable but at the same time may have social, cultural and political capacities to cope with disasters. Risk reduction strategies for the poor should work towards reducing economic vulnerability and at the same time capitalise on (and perhaps nurture) the inherent social and cultural capacities of poor communities. It is imperative that while improving the economic resilience of such communities, physical, social and political risks are also recognised and managed.

There is another aspect of vulnerability of the poor, which is frequently ignored: it is often local in nature. Disaster statistics collected and aggregated at provincial and national levels do not capture the miseries of the poor and the most vulnerable. Impact assessments capture only the formal and well-defined sectors of the economy. It is becoming clear that the nature of vulnerability of the poor is complex and varied. Hence, reducing risk to the poor will require multidimensional approaches and innovative institutional arrangements.

Integrating Poverty Reduction Programmes with the Disaster Management Sector

There have been relatively few examples of systematic integration of poverty reduction and disaster reduction programmes. There are three approaches that have evolved over the last several years. *First,* is the livelihood framework developed in the context of bilateral development aid. *Second* is community-based disaster management, evolved in the disaster management sector. *Third,* are specific financial instruments to deal with risk transfer, encouraged by multilateral agencies. An integrated approach using the three perspectives is best to address disaster preparedness and management.

Recognising the Vulnerability Context of the Poor within the Development Framework

A more holistic framework to assess the sustainability of livelihood strategies adopted by poor people has emerged over the last few years. The work of Sustainable Rural Livelihoods Advisory Committee of the British

Department for International Development (DFID) is a good example. The Committee has designed a livelihood framework, which recognises five distinct elements of interactions that determine the degree of sustainability of livelihood strategies of a particular community. These five elements are:

(i) Vulnerability context of poor people;

(ii) Their livelihood assets (human, social, physical, natural and financial capital);

(iii) Transforming structures (government, private sector) and processes (laws, institutions);

(iv) Livelihood strategies; and

(v) Livelihood outcomes.

This approach captures the dynamic, complex nature of people's vulnerability. The vulnerability context frames the external environment including trends (population trends, resource trends), shocks (natural hazards, disease outbreak), and seasonality (market prices, employment opportunities). This framework does not look at the vulnerability context in isolation, but links it with transforming structures and processes. Practical application of such a framework means that it not only describes the different aspects of people's vulnerability but also points to social, political and economic structures and processes, transformations that would help reduce vulnerability, and thus help insure sustainable livelihood for the poor.

Disasters adversely affect the livelihoods of poor people by damaging their means of earning (destruction of the factory, loss of land due to erosion in flooding, destruction of the shop) and/or tools (loss of draught animals, plowing tools, etc). Mainstream disaster management responses frequently neglect the rehabilitation of people's means of livelihood. Families, who lose their means of livelihood during a disaster, find their recovery from adverse effects becoming more unlikely and their vulnerability to future disasters increased. It is also assumed that if people have better sources of livelihoods and higher incomes, they will spend more on disaster risk management in order to save their property because, due to higher incomes, they have savings to spend for this purpose. If, however, they do not have savings, spending on disaster management becomes the lowest priority in comparison to the chronic issues of survival. Diversity in the source of livelihoods is very important for increasing people's capacity to cope and recover. If a family, for example, has two different sources of income, a tract of land and a shop, the family still has the shop if it were to lose a draught animal or a crop. The family will obviously be in a better position than a family that has only one tract of land and loses the standing crop.

Investment in strengthening and diversifying the sources of livelihoods of people in disaster prone areas can thus be an effective strategy for disaster risk reduction in the long run. The Asian Disaster Preparedness Center (ADPC) has been involved in such initiatives in various countries of the South Asian region in collaboration with its partners.

Community-Based Disaster Management

Top-down management approaches were simply unsuccessful in addressing the needs of vulnerable communities. A better understanding of disasters and losses reveals that the increase in disaster occurrence and disaster related loss is due to the exponential increase in occurrence of small and medium scale disasters. As a result many feel it is important to adopt a newstrategy, which directly involves vulnerable people themselves in planning and implementation of mitigation measures.

This bottom-up approach has received wide acceptance because communities are considered the best judges of their own vulnerability and can make the best decisions regarding their own well-being. What is the community-based disaster management (CBDM) approach? The aim of CBDM is to reduce vulnerabilities and strengthen people's capacity to cope with hazards. A thorough assessment of a community's exposure to hazards and an analysis of their specific vulnerabilities and capacities is the basis for activities, projects and programmes that can reduce disaster risks. Because a community is involved in the whole process, their felt and real needs, as well as inherent resources, are considered. It is therefore more likely that appropriate interventions will be used.

People's participation concerns both processes and content. The community should be able to gain directly from improved disaster risk management. This, in turn, will contribute to a progression towards safer conditions, security of livelihood and sustainable development. This underlines the point that the community is not only the primary actor but also the beneficiary of the risk reduction and development process. Some authors differentiate between community participation and involvement. Community participation is generally taken to mean that a given community takes responsibility at all stages of a programme, including planning and implementation. Community involvement refers to a 'less than' ideal situation, where the community is asked to participate in a programme that has already been designed by someone else.

Implementation of CBDM points to the following essential features:

(i) The community's central role. The focus of attention in long-term and short-term disaster management must be the local community.

(ii) Disaster risk or vulnerability reduction as the foundation of CBDM. The primary content of disaster management activities revolve around reducing vulnerable conditions and the root causes of vulnerability. The primary strategy of vulnerability reduction is to increase a community's capacities, resources and coping strategies.

(iii) Linkage to the development process. Disasters are viewed as unmanaged development risks and unresolved problems of the development process. CBDM should lead to a general improvement of the quality of life of the vast majority of the poor people and of the natural environment. CBDM contributes to people's empowerment-to possess physical safety; to have more access and control of resources; to participate in decisionmaking that affects their lives; to enjoy the benefits of a healthy environment.

(iv) Community as a key resource in disaster risk reduction. The community is the key actor as well as the primary beneficiary of disaster risk reduction. Within the community, priority attention is given to the conditions of the most vulnerable as well as to their mobilisation in disaster risk reduction. The community participates in the whole process of disaster risk management from situational analysis to planning to implementation.

(v) Application of multisectoral and multidisciplinary approaches. CBDM brings together the multitude of community stakeholders for disaster risk reduction to expand its resource base. The local community level links up with the intermediate and national and even up to the international level to address the complexity of vulnerability issues. A wide range of approaches to disaster risk reduction is employed.

(vi) CBDM as an involving and dynamic framework. Lessons learned from practice continue to build into the theory of CBDM. The sharing of experiences, methodologies and tools by communities and CBDM practitioners continues to enrich practice.

Before implementing CBDM it is important to know who in the community should be involved. The most vulnerable are the primary actors in a community. The focus should be at the household level. As all individuals, houses, organisations and services stand a chance of being affected, they should all be involved. But before working on disaster risk reduction, differing perceptions, interests, and methodologies have to be recognised and a broad consensus on targets, strategies and methodologies have to be reached. To enrich the community's involvement in risk reduction, it is important to first assess the risk with the help of the community. There are specific tools and methods that can make the process of community risk assessment most effective.

There are a number of strategies for community-based risk reduction:

(i) Self-insurance options:

— Reinforcing people's existing livelihoods to increase or maintain current level of production and income-draft animal dispersal, irrigation (expansion, improvement in water management), soil fertility improvement, and seed and livestock dispersal. This strategy seems to be effective for internal refugees returning to their abandoned lands, for former farm workers who cultivate and expand their occupied lands, and in cases where irrigation systems can be rehabilitated after earthquakes, floods and typhoons. The effect is that the period of food shortage is reduced by several months.

— Reinforcing people's coping strategies to reduce risks. This means diversifying crops, the promotion and production of disaster resistant and other indigenous crops. In this case, if one crop fails, the other will survive.

— Strengthening social and organisational support structures, and improving post-harvest facilities and storage methods. This will result in increased reserves of food at household/ community level; therefore the number of food shortage months is reduced.

(ii) Conducting seasonally based action. Several disasters are seasonal in nature. Effective methods to combat these disasters are develop seasonal cycles of preparedness, such as planting of disaster resistant crops, storage and post-harvest facilities, seed banks, and mobile resources.

(iii) Encouraging long-term investments, which are fallback resources in the community. Examples are: forest reserves, planting of trees around the house, establishment of village pharmacy, training of village health workers, education or functional literacy, all of which are long term investments. They reduce people's long-term vulnerability. It involves land use and management planning within the community.

(iv) Strengthening social and organisational support structures to establish a community spirit of cooperation, through organisational development and management, counter disaster planning, disaster response committee formation, leadership training, functional literacy, day care services, etc. These support mechanisms help in terms of better

decision-making and managing community wide activities for evacuation and emergency response.

(v) Making health and sanitation services available at the community level, through capacity building of the community workers: make first aid, mother and child care, supplementary feeding for malnourished children, promotion of low cost nutrition food, education and awareness generation for better hygiene and sanitation conditions. These will reduce risks of disease and epidemics.

(vi) Conducting advocacy and information campaigns to press government, from the local to the national level, continually regarding policies and issues that affect the local food security and nutrition situation and/or that form a barrier to solve the problems. It would stop external threats. Harmful policies and action are blocked.

Risk Transfer and Finance

Appropriate public policy interventions are very important for reducing socioeconomic vulnerabilities. Increased access to resources, increased employment opportunities, increasing macroeconomic stability, and other conscious policies made to improve quality of life, are necessary. Households may access the risks pools through a variety of formal and informal arrangements, which are determined by the nature of the risks and transaction costs associated with drawing on the pool. Improved and innovative financial instruments that provide households access to financial resources and thus help in reducing, sharing and transferring of risks are important. Options are:

(i) *Mitigation/vulnerability reduction fund:* Emergency funds usually given to households after a disaster should be used to reduce risks. It can be used to

subsidize insurance in an area or encourage re-insurance. Governments can withdraw this facility once the situation has improved and the insurance companies can manage the risk exposure.

(ii) *Self-insurance:* Households can take a conscious decision to share some risk of loss. By agreeing to share losses, individuals and companies become conscious of the need to implement mitigation measures.

(iii) *Group-based insurance programmes:* A group based insurance programme can enlarge a risk pool and provide insurance at an affordable price. According to Kreimer, et al., a large number of policy holders *(a)* reduces the potential of adverse selection-in which claims are higher than expected because only high risk households purchase the insurance and *(b)* increases the likelihood that the variance of actual claims will be closer to the expected mean used in calculating premiums. Other advantages of group insurance are that it is faster to get membership by insuring groups rather than individuals, it also reduces the cost of administration, it provides appropriate mitigation incentives to the community—people come together and initiate improvements in their physical surroundings in order to qualify for the insurance.

(iv) *Microcredits:* Microfinance and rural banks are important sources of credit for the poor. However such an institution may be overwhelmed with credit demands at the time of a disaster.

(v) *Informal credit markets:* These credits are repaid based on a random schedule of production. Free flow of information in this informal system helps in the process of scheduling repayments, fixing interest rates and plays a direct role in insuring against the risk. This system is effective at protecting households from risks but not at the village level.

(vi) *Natural disaster insurance:* Disaster insurance spreads the risk over a larger group, provides better-cost efficiency, discriminates between the needs of the different insured people, encourages loss reduction measures as a condition of insurance, and it also monitors the activities of the insured.

COMMUNITY-BASED DISASTER RISK REDUCTION PROCESS

Community-based disaster management is a risk reduction measure. The disaster risk reduction process has six sequential stages, which can be operationalised before a disaster occurs or after one has happened to reduce future risks. Each stage grows out of the preceding stage and leads to further action. Together, the sequence can build up a planning and implementation system, which can become a powerful disaster risk reduction tool. The stages in the risk reduction process are as follows:

(i) Initiating the disaster risk reduction process.

(ii) Community Profiling.

(iii) Community Risk Assessment.

(iv) Community Risk Reduction Planning.

(v) Implementation and Monitoring.

(vi) Evaluation and Feedback.

Initiating the Disaster Reduction Process

In some cases, several community members or an organisation in the community approaches an intermediary organisation for assistance after experiencing a disaster or in preparing for an impending disaster threat. NGOs, disaster management agencies, the government and other intermediary organisations such as national or regional level people's organisations can play a key role in initiating the process of community-based disaster management. They either respond to requests coming from vulnerable communities or identify vulnerable communities where disaster risk reduction programmes should be prioritised.

Criteria for the prioritisation of vulnerable communities may include the following: most disaster prone area; most vulnerable to a particular hazard; least served by the government and/or NGOs; and additional considerations such as possibility of replication or spread effects of the programme to neighboring communities, presence of existing development projects or community partners. In many instances, a probable hazard event or disaster threat can be turned into an opportunity to start a community-based disaster management programme. When the knowledge, skills and experiences in disaster risk reduction, which are in communities are systematised and disseminated, there will be more community-to-community sharing on how to get started and implement community-based disaster management.

Community Profiling

Community profiling involves building up a picture of the nature, needs and resources of a community with the active participation of the community. It is an important preliminary step in any planning process, especially when outsiders (intermediary organisations) are involved. It usually involves building rapport/ trust with the community through interaction and gathering basic information or the surfacing of the general community profile. It leads to an understanding of the community's development position and the context upon which disasters will impact. Basic elements of a community profile will include the following: social groups, cultural arrangements, economic activities, spatial characteristics, vulnerable households and groups.

Community Risk Assessment

Community risk assessment is a diagnostic process to balance known disaster risks against available resources. Through the risk assessment process, the community comes to a common understanding of its disaster risks. The size of the problem as well as the resources and opportunities involved are identified and analysed. Community risk assessment has four components as follows:

(i) Hazard assessment.

(ii) Vulnerability assessment.

(iii) Capacity assessment.

(iv) People's perception of the risks.

Formulation of Disaster Risk Reduction Plan

Preparedness and mitigation measures to reduce disaster risks are identified. These risk reduction measures are not necessarily big projects. The important point is to start off the risk reduction process through community mobilisation based on existing capacities and resources within the community's immediate reach. Overall objectives, strategies are translated to operational plans and activities. Responsible people, timetable, resources within and outside the community needed to turn the intent of the plan into reality are identified. Community targets in undertaking preparedness and mitigation measures in terms of particular capacities increased and vulnerabilities decreased are also identified.

At the planning stage, agreements with intermediary organisations are formalised regarding their supports in the risk reduction plan implementation and their expectations/requirements of resources, which they commit to mobilise. Outsiders are usually expected to assist the community in the following areas: *(i)* community capability building through training and education activities and materials; *(ii)* resource mobilisation to supplement the community's efforts to generate resources to realise the risk reduction plan; and *(iii)* facilitate linkages with concerned government agencies and NGOs to access information, resources, etc.

Implementation and Monitoring

The formation and/or strengthening of community disaster management machinery is usually helpful in the implementation of the risk reduction plan. A wide range of organisational arrangements vital in implementation of the plan include the following-a committee of an existing community organisation, a disaster volunteer team, a community organisation, a project management committee, a network of community organisations for disaster management, etc. Besides monitoring the progress of the plan implementation, this core group motivates the community through translation of plan objectives and targets into disaster reduction activities. This group also amends targets and plans, when necessary, to keep on course with set objectives to reduce vulnerabilities and increase capacities in the immediate and long-term.

Evaluations and Feedback

Evaluation is concerned with the effects of the risk reduction measures in terms of reducing the vulnerability situation of the community. If vulnerability has not been significantly reduced, the reasons for this are analysed. The significance of building on existing capacities and those, which have been actually increased, are also analysed. It is concerned with the difference the results of the risk reduction measures have made to the community situation and its overall quality of life.

9

Disaster Prevention Programmes and Policies in India

Over the past couple of years, the Government of India have brought about a paradigm shift in the approach to disaster management. The new approach proceeds from the conviction that development cannot be sustainable unless disaster mitigation is built into the development process. Another corner stone of the approach is that mitigation has to be multi-disciplinary spanning across all sectors of development. The new policy also emanates from the belief that investments in mitigation are much more cost effective than expenditure on relief and rehabilitation.

Disaster management occupies an important place in this country's policy framework as it is the poor and the under-privileged who are worst affected on account of calamities/disasters. The approach has been translated into a National Disaster Framework [a roadmap] covering institutional mechanisms, disaster prevention strategy, early warning system, disaster mitigation, preparedness and response and human resource development. The expected inputs, areas of intervention and agencies to be involved at the National, State and district levels have been identified and listed in the roadmap. This roadmap has been shared with all the State Governments and Union Territory Administrations. Ministries and Departments of Government of India, and the State Governments/UT Administrations have been advised to develop their respective roadmaps taking the national roadmap as a broad guideline. There is, therefore, now a common strategy underpinning the action being taken by all the participating organisations/stakeholders.

INSTITUTIONAL AND POLICY FRAMEWORK

The institutional and policy mechanisms for carrying out response, relief and rehabilitation have been well-established since Independence. These mechanisms have proved to be robust and effective insofar as response, relief and rehabilitation are concerned.

At the national level, the Ministry of Home Affairs is the nodal Ministry for all matters concerning disaster management. The Central Relief Commissioner (CRC) in the Ministry of Home Affairs is the nodal officer to coordinate relief operations for natural disasters. The CRC receives information relating to forecasting/warning of a natural calamity from India Meteorological Department (IMD) or from Central Water Commission of Ministry of Water Resources on a continuing basis. The Ministries/Departments/Organisations concerned with the primary and secondary functions relating to the management of disasters include: Meteorological Department of India Central Water Commission, Ministry of Home Affairs, Ministry of Defence, Ministry of Finance, Ministry of Rural Development, Ministry of Urban Development, Department of Communications, Ministry of Health, Ministry of Water Resources, Ministry of Petroleum, Department of Agriculture & Cooperation. Ministry of Power, Department of Civil Supplies, Ministry of Railways, Ministry of Information and

Broadcasting, Planning Commission, Cabinet Secretariat, Department of Surface Transport, Ministry of Social Justice, Department of Women and Child Development, Ministry of Environment and Forest, Department of Food. Each Ministry/Department/Organisation nominate their nodal officer to the Crisis Management Group chaired by Central Relief Commissioner. The nodal officer is responsible for preparing sectoral Action Plan/ Emergency Support Function Plan for managing disasters.

National Crisis Management Committee (NCMC): Cabinet Secretary, who is the highest executive officer, heads the NCMC. Secretaries of all the concerned Ministries/Departments as well as organisations are the members of the Committee The NCMC gives direction to the Crisis Management Group as deemed necessary. The Secretary, Ministry of Home Affairs is responsible for ensuring that all developments are brought to the notice of the NCMC promptly. The NCMC can give directions to any Ministry/Department/Organisation for specific action needed for meeting the crisis situation.

Crisis Management Group: The Central Relief Commissioner in the Ministry of Home Affairs is the Chairman of the CMG, consisting of senior officers (called nodal officers) from various concerned ministries. The CMG's functions are to review every year contingency plans formulated by various Ministries/ Departments/Organisations in their respective sectors, measures required for dealing with a natural disasters, coordinate the activities of the Central Ministries and the State Governments in relation to disaster preparedness and relief and to obtain information from the nodal officers on measures relating to above. The CMG, in the event of a natural disaster, meets frequently to review the relief operations and extend all possible assistance required by the affected States to overcome the situation effectively. The Resident Commissioner of the affected State is also associated with such meetings.

Control Room (Emergency Operation Room): An Emergency Operations Center (Control Room) exists in the nodal Ministry of Home Affairs, which functions round the clock, to assist the Central Relief Commissioner in the discharge of his duties. The activities of the Control Room include collection and transmission of information concerning natural calamity and relief, keeping close contact with governments of the affected States, interaction with other Central Ministries/Departments/ Organisations in connection with relief, maintaining records containing all relevant information relating to action points and contact points in Central Ministries etc., keeping up-to-date details of all concerned officers at the Central and State levels. Contingency Action Plan: A National Contingency Action Plan (CAP) for dealing with contingencies arising in the wake of natural disasters has been formulated by the Government of India and it had been periodically updated. It facilitates the launching of relief operations without delay. The CAP identifies the initiatives required to be taken by various Central Ministries/Departments in the wake of natural calamities, sets down the procedure and determines the focal points in the administrative machinery.

State Relief Manuals: Each State Government has relief manuals/codes which identify that role of each officer in the State for managing the natural disasters. These are reviewed and updated periodically based on the experience of managing the disasters and the need of the State.

Funding mechanisms: The policy and the funding mechanism for provision of relief assistance to those affected by natural calamities is clearly laid down. These are reviewed by the Finance Commission appointed by the Government of India every five years. The Finance Commission makes recommendation regarding the division of tax and non-tax revenues between the Central and the State Governments and also regarding policy for provision of relief assistance and their share of expenditure thereon. A Calamity Relief Fund (CRF) has been set up in each State as per the recommendations of the Eleventh Finance Commission. The size of the Calamity Relief Fund has been fixed by the Finance Commission after taking into account the expenditure on relief and rehabilitation over the past 10 years. The Government of India contributes 75% of the corpus of the Calamity Relief Fund in each State. 25% is contributed to by the State. Relief assistance to those affected by natural calamities is granted from the CRF. Overall norms for relief assistance are laid down by a national committee with representatives of States as members. Different States can have Statespecific norms to be recommended by State level committee under the Chief Secretary. Where the calamity is of such proportion that the funds available in the CRF will not be sufficient for provision of relief, the State seeks assistance from the National Calamity Contingency Fund (NCCF) — a fund created at the Central Government level. When such requests are received, the requirements are assessed by a team from the Central Government and thereafter the assessed requirements are cleared by a High Level Committee chaired by the Deputy Prime Minister. In brief, the institutional arrangements for response and relief are wellestablished and have proved to be robust and effective.

In the federal set up of India, the basic responsibility for undertaking rescue, relief and rehabilitation measures in the event of a disaster is that of the State Government concerned. At the State level, response, relief and rehabilitation are handled by Departments of Relief &

Rehabilitation. The State Crisis Management Committee set up under the Chairmanship of Chief Secretary who is the highest executive functionary in the State. All the concerned Departments and organisations of the State and Central Government Departments located in the State are represented in this Committee. This Committee reviews the action taken for response and relief and gives guidelines/directions as necessary. A control room is established under the Relief Commissioner. The control room is in constant touch with the climate monitoring/forecasting agencies and monitors the action being taken by various agencies in performing their responsibilities. The district level is the key level for disaster management and relief activities. The Collector/Dy. Commissioner is the chief administrator in the district. He is the focal point in the preparation of district plans and in directing, supervising and monitoring calamities for relief. A District Level Coordination and Relief Committee is constituted and is headed by the Collector as Chairman with participation of all other related government and non governmental agencies and departments in addition to the elected representatives. The Collector is required to maintain close liaison with the district and the State Governments as well as the nearest units of Armed Forces/Central police organisations and other relevant Central Government organisations like Ministries of Communications, Water Resources, Drinking Water, Surface Transport, who could supplement the efforts of the district administration in the rescue and relief operations. The efforts of the Government and non-governmental organisations for response and relief and coordinated by the Collector/Dy. Commissioner. The District Magistrate/Collector and Coordination Committee under him reviews preparedness measures prior to a impending hazard and coordinate response when the hazard strikes. As all the Departments of the

State Government and district level report to the Collector, there is an effective coordination mechanism ensuring holistic response.

New institutional mechanisms: As has been made clear above, the existing mechanisms had based on post-disaster relief and rehabilitation and they have proved to be robust and effective mechanisms in addressing these requirements. The changed policy/approach, however, mandates a priority to full disaster aspects of mitigation, prevention and preparedness and new institutional and policy mechanisms are being put in place to address the policy change.

It is proposed to constitute a National Emergency Management Authority at the National level. The High Powered Committee on Disaster Management which was set up in August, 1999 and submitted its Report in October, 2001, had inter alia recommended that a separate Department of Disaster Management be set up in the Government of India. It was, however, felt that conventional Ministries/Departments have the drawback of not being flexible enough specially in terms of the sanction procedures. The organisation at the Apex level will have to be multi-disciplinary with experts covering a large number of branches. The National Emergency Management Authority has, therefore, been proposed as a combined Secretariat/Directorate structure — a structure which will be an integral part of the Government and, therefore, will work with the full authority of the Government while, at the same time, retaining the flexibility of a field organisation. The National Emergency Management Authority will be headed by an officer of the rank of Secretary/Special Secretary to the Government in the Ministry of Home Affairs with Special Secretaries/Additional Secretaries from the Ministries/Departments of Health, Water Resources, Environment & Forests, Agriculture, Railways,

Atomic Energy, Defence, Chemicals, Science & Technology, Telecommunications, Urban Employment and Poverty Alleviation, Rural Development and India Meteorological Department as Members of the Authority. The Authority would meet as often as required and review the status of warning systems, mitigation measures and disaster preparedness. When a disaster strikes, the Authority will coordinate disaster management activities. The Authority will be responsible for:

(i) Coordinating/mandating Government's policies for disaster reduction/mitigation.

(ii) Ensuring adequate preparedness at all levels in order to meet disasters.

(iii) Coordinating response to a disaster when it strikes.

(iv) Coordination of post disaster relief and rehabilitation.

The National Emergency Management Authority will have a core permanent secretariat with three divisions — one for Disaster Prevention, Mitigation & Rehabilitation, the other for Preparedness and the third for Human Resource Development.

At the State level, as indicated in para disaster management was being handled by the Departments of Relief & Rehabilitation. As the name suggests, the focus was almost entirely on post-calamity relief. The Government of India is working with the State Governments to convert the Departments of Relief & Rehabilitation into Departments of Disaster Management with an enhanced area of responsibility to include mitigation and preparedness apart from their present responsibilities of relief and rehabilitation. The change over has already happened in eight State Governments/ Union Territory Administrations. The change is under process in other States.

The States have also been asked to set up Disaster Management Authorities under the Chief Minister with Ministers of relevant Departments [Water Resources, Agriculture, Drinking Water Supply, Environment & Forests, Urban Development, Home, Rural Development etc.] as members. The objective of setting up an Authority is to ensure that mitigation and preparedness is seen as the joint responsibility of all the Departments concerned and disaster management concerns are mainstreamed into their programmes. This holistic and multidisciplinary approach is the key to effective mitigation.

At the district level, the District Magistrate who is the chief coordinator will be the focal point for coordinating all activities relating to prevention, mitigation and preparedness apart from his existing responsibilities pertaining to response and relief. The District Coordination and Relief Committee is being reconstituted/ re-designated into Disaster Management Committees with officers from relevant departments being added as members. Because of its enhanced mandate of mitigation and prevention, the district heads and departments engaged in development will now be added to the Committee so that mitigation and prevention is mainstreamed into the district plan. The existing system of drawing up preparedness and response plans will continue. There will, however, also be a long term mitigation plan. District Disaster Management Committees have already been constituted in several districts and are in the process of being constituted in the remaining multi-hazard prone districts.

Similarly, we are in the process of creating Block/ Taluq Disaster Management Committees in these 169 multi-hazard prone districts in 17 States. At the village level, in 169 multi-hazard prone districts, we are constituting Disaster Management Committees and Disaster Management Teams. Each village will have a

Disaster Management Plan. The process of drafting the plan has already begun. The Disaster Management Committee which draws up the plans consists of elected representatives at the village level, local authorities, Government functionaries including doctors/paramedics of primary health centres located in the village, primary school teachers etc. The plan encompasses prevention, mitigation and preparedness measures. The Disaster Management Teams at the village level will consist of members of voluntary organisations like Nehru Yuvak Kendra and other non-governmental organisations as well as able bodied volunteers from the village. The teams are provided basic training in evacuation, search and rescue etc. The Disaster Management Committee will review the disaster management plan at least once in a year. It would also generate awareness among the people in the village about dos' and don'ts for specific hazards depending on the vulnerability of the village. A large number of village level Disaster Management Committees and Disaster Management Teams have already been constituted.

The States have been advised to enact Disaster Management Acts. These Acts provide for adequate powers for authorities coordinating mitigation, preparedness and response as well as for mitigation/ prevention measures required to be undertaken. Two States [Gujarat and Madhya Pradesh] have already enacted such a law. Other States are in the process. The State Governments have also been advised to convert their Relief Codes into Disaster Management Codes by including aspects of prevention, mitigation and preparedness. In order to further institutionalise the new approach, the Government of India have decided to enunciate a National Policy on Disaster Management. A draft policy has accordingly been formulated and is expected to be put in place shortly. The policy shall inform all spheres of Central Government activity and shall take precedence over all existing sectoral policies. The broad objectives of the policy are to minimise the loss of lives and social, private and community assets because of natural or manmade disasters and contribute to sustainable development and better standards of living for all, more specifically for the poor and vulnerable sections by ensuring that the development gains are not lost through natural calamities/disasters.

The policy notes that State Governments are primarily responsible for disaster management including prevention and mitigation, while the Government of India provides assistance where necessary as per the norms laid down from time to time and proposes that this overall framework may continue. However, since response to a disaster requires coordination of resources available across all the Departments of the Government, the policy mandates that the Central Government will, in conjunction with the State Governments, seek to ensure that such a coordination mechanism is laid down through an appropriate chain of command so that mobilisation of resources is facilitated.

The broad features of the draft national policy on disaster management are enunciated below:

(i) A holistic and pro-active approach for prevention, mitigation and preparedness will be adopted for disaster management.

(ii) Each Ministry/Department of the Central/State Government will set apart an appropriate quantum of funds under the Plan for specific schemes/ projects addressing vulnerability reduction and preparedness.

(iii) Where there is a shelf of projects, projects addressing mitigation will be given priority. Mitigation measures shall be built into the on-going schemes/programmes.

(iv) Each project in a hazard prone area will have mitigation as an essential term of reference. The project report will include a statement as to how the project addresses vulnerability reduction.

(v) Community involvement and awareness generation, particularly that of the vulnerable segments of population and women has been emphasised as necessary for sustainable disaster risk reduction. This is a critical component of the policy since communities are the first responders to disasters and, therefore, unless they are empowered and made capable of managing disasters, any amount of external support cannot lead to optimal results.

(vi) There will be close interaction with the corporate sector, non-governmental organisations and the media in the national efforts for disaster prevention/vulnerability reduction.

(vii) Institutional structures/appropriate chain of command will be built up and appropriate training imparted to disaster managers at various levels to ensure coordinated and quick response at all levels; and development of inter-State arrangements for sharing of resources during emergencies.

(viii) A culture of planning and preparedness is to be inculcated at all levels for capacity building measures.

(ix) Standard operating procedures and disaster management plans at state and district levels as well as by relevant central government departments for handling specific disasters will be laid down.

(x) Construction designs must correspond to the requirements as laid down in relevant Indian Standards.

(xi) All lifeline buildings in seismic zones III, IV & V—hospitals, railway stations, airports/airport control towers, fire station buildings, bus stands major administrative centres will need to be evaluated and, if necessary, retro-fitted.

(xii) The existing relief codes in the States will be revised to develop them into disaster management codes/manuals for institutionalising the planning process with particular attention to mitigation and preparedness.

With the above mentioned institutional mechanism and policy framework in position and the actions taken to implement the policy guidelines, it is expected that the task of moving towards vulnerability reduction will be greatly facilitated.

EARLY WARNING SYSTEM

Cyclone Forecasting

Tropical Cyclones are intense low pressure systems which develop over warm sea. They are capable of causing immense damage due to strong winds, heavy rains and storm surges. The frequency of the TC in the Bay of Bengal is 4 to 5 times more than in the Arabian Sea. About 35% of initial disturbances in the north Indian ocean reach TC stage of which 45% become severe. Indian Meteorological Department (IMD) is mandated to monitor and give warnings regarding Tropical Cyclone (TC). Monitoring process has been revolutionised by the advent of remote sensing techniques. A TC intensity analysis and forecast scheme has been worked out using satellite image interpretation techniques which facilitate forecasting of storm surges. Data resources are crucial to early forecasting of cyclones. Satellite based observations are being extensively utilised. Satellite integrated automated weather stations have been installed on islands, oilrigs and exposed coastal sites. Buoys for supplementing the surface data network in the tropical ocean have been deployed. The Government have also started a National Data Buoy Programme. A set of 12 moored buoys have been deployed in the northern Indian Ocean to provide meteorological and oceanographic data.

Dynamic forecasting of TCs requires knowledge of the vertical structure of both the Cyclone and the surrounding environment. The rawin sonde remains the principal equipment for sounding. The Doppler Radar wind profiler provides hourly soundings. A mesosphere, stratosphere, troposphere (MST) radar has also been installed at Thirupatti. Another profiler is being developed and will be deployed at IMD Pune. Another important source of upper level data is the aircraft reports. Increasing number of commercial jet aircraft are equipped with the Aircraft Meteorological Data Relay system. This data is being made available is also being used by the IMD for analysis and predictions. Radars have been used to observe TCs since long. Surveillance of the spiral rain bands and the eye of the TC is an important function of the coastal radars. 10 Cyclones Detection Radars have already been installed. These radars are providing useful estimates of storm centres upto a range 300-400 km. Doppler radars provide direct measurements of wind fields in TCs. Due to range limitation, Doppler wind estimates are usually within a range of about 100 Km. IMD has deployed Doppler radars at 3 sites on the east coast. Another set of 3 Doppler radars are being deployed in Andhra Pradesh in near future.

The meteorological satellite has made a tremendous impact on the analysis of cyclones. All developing cloud clusters are routinely observed through satellite cloud imagery & those showing signs of organisation are closely monitored for signs of intensification. TC forecasters everywhere use the Dvorak technique to estimate storm location and intensity. It has been found to provide realistic estimates for TCs in the Bay of Bengal as well as Arabian Sea. INSAT data has also been used to study the structures of different TCs in the Bay of Bengal. IMD is also producing Cloud Motion Vectors (CMVs). Very High Resolution Radiometer (VHRR) payload onboard INSAT-2E which have been improved upon to provide water vapor channel data in addition to VIS & IR onboard INSAT-2E. A separate payload known as Charged Couple Device (CCD) has also been deployed onboard this satellite.

The goal of any warning system is to maximise the number of people who take appropriate and timely action for the safety of life and property. All warning systems start with detection of the event and with people getting out of harm's way. Such warning systems encompass three equally important elements namely; Detection and Warning; Communication; and Response.

The two stage warning system has been in existence since long in IMD. Recently it has been improved upon by introducing two more stages — the 'Pre-Cyclone watch' and the 'post-landfall Scenario'. This four stage warning system meets the requirements of Public Administrators and Crisis Managers. The 'Pre-Cyclone Watch' stage, contains early warning about the development of a cyclonic disturbance in the form of monsoon depression which has a potential to threaten the coast with cyclone force winds. The coastal stretch likely to be affected is identified. This early warning bulletin is issued by the IMD before the Cyclone-Alert Stage. This provides enough lead time for the crisis managers to undertake preparedness actions.

After the early warning on the 'Pre-Cyclone Watch' the Collectors of coastal and few immediate interior districts and the Chief Secretary of the concerned maritime State are warned in two stages, whenever any coastal belt is expected to experience adverse weather (heavy rain/gales/tidal wave) in association with a cyclonic storm or a depression likely to intensify into a cyclonic storm.

The second stage of "Cyclone Alert" is sounded 48 hours in advance of the expected commencement of adverse weather over the coastal areas. Forecasts of commencement of strong winds, heavy precipitation along the coast in association with arrival of cyclone are issued at the alert stage. Landfall point is usually not identified at this stage. The third stage warning known as "Cyclone Warning" is issued 24 hours in advance. Landfall point is forecast in this stage of cyclone warning. In addition to the forecasts for heavy rains and strong winds, the storm surge forecast is also issued. Since the storm surge is the biggest killer so far as the devastating attributes of a storm are concerned, information in this regard is most critical for taking follow up action for evacuation from the low lying areas likely to be affected by the storm. After the landfall of the cyclone the strong winds with gale force speeds continue over certain interior districts of the maritime States hit by the cyclone.

To take cognizance of that, a fourth stage known as 'Post-landfall Scenario Stage' is now identified usually as a part of the 'Cyclone Warning Stage' either at the time of landfall of the disturbance or about twelve hour in advance of it. It includes warnings of strong winds and heavy rains likely to be encountered in the interior districts.

For communications, the IMD makes use of 97 point-to-point teleprinter links connecting different field offices.

Switching computers have been provided at 5 Regional Centres. These computers are linked to the Central Regional Telecom Hub Computer at New Delhi. In addition, 69 centres have been provided with 85 telex connections. Besides, 27 field offices have been provided with Radio Teletype facility. IMD also utilises VSAT technology which has been installed at field offices. In addition, there are a number of HF/RT and VHF links.

Cyclone warnings are communicated to Crisis Managers and other concerned organisations by high priority telegrams, telex, telephones and Police wireless. Cyclone warning are provided by the IMD from the Area Cyclone Warning Centres (ACWCs) at Kalkata, Chennai and Mumbai and Cyclone Warning Centres (CWCs) at Vishakhapatnam, Bhubaneswar and Ahmedabad. There is also a Satellite based communication system called the Cyclone Warning Dissemination Systems (CWDS) for transmission of warnings. There are 250 such cyclone-warning sets installed in the cylone prone areas of east and west coast. The general public, the coastal residents and fishermen, are also warned through the Government mechinery and broadcast of warnings through AIR and Television.

Flood Forecasting

Flooding is caused by the inadequate capacity within the banks of the rivers to contain the high flow brought down from the upper catchments due to heavy rainfall. It is also caused by accumulation of water resulting from heavy spells of rainfall over areas, which have got poor drainage characteristics. Flooding is accentuated by erosion and silting leading to meandering of the rivers in plains and reduction in carrying capacity of the river channel. It is also aggravated by earthquakes and land slides, leading to changes in river course and obstructions to flow. Synchronisation of floods in the main rivers and tributaries and retardation of flow due to tidal effects lead to major floods. Cyclones bring in their wake considerable loss of life and property. The flood forecasting and warning system is used for alerting the likely damage centers well in advance of the actual arrival of floods, to enable the people to move and also to remove the moveable property to safer places or to raised platforms specially constructed for the purpose.

A beginning in scientific flood forecasting was made in November, 1958 by Central Water Commission (then known as Central Water & Power Commission) when a Flood Forecasting Centre was set up at its Headquarters, at New Delhi, for giving timely Forecasts and Warnings of the incoming floods to the villages located in the river areas around the National Capital, Delhi. The network has been expanding and by now the Flood Forecasting Network of the Central Water Commission (CWC) covers all the major flood prone inter-State river basins in the country.

At present there are 166 flood forecasting stations on various rivers in the country which includes 134 level forecasting and 32 inflow forecasting stations.

The Flood Forecasting involves the following four main activities:

(i) Observation and collection of hydrological and hydro-meteorological data;

(ii) Transmission of Data to Forecasting Centres;

(iii) Analysis of data and formulation of forecast; and

(iv) Dissemination of forecast.

On an average, 6000 forecasts at various places in the country are issued during the monsoon season every year. The analysis of the forecasts issued during the last 25 years (1978 to 2002) indicates that accuracy of forecasts has consistently increased from around 81% to 98%.

Forecast is considered accurate if forecast water level is within ± 15 cm. of actual water level of the inflow forecast (i.e. discharge) is with in ± 20% of actual discharge. 3.25 In monitoring the floods, severity of floods are placed in the following four categories by the central Water Commissions.

(i) *Low flood stage:* It is that flood situation when the water level of the river is flowing between warning level and danger level of the forecasting stations.

(ii) *Medium flood stage:* The river is called in medium floods when its water level is at or above the danger level of the forecasting station but below 0.50 of its highest flood level (HFL).

(iii) *High flood stage:* When the water level of the river is below the HFL but within 0.50 m. of the HFL of the forecasting stations.

(iv) *Unprecedented flood stage:* The river is called in unprecedented floods when it attains water level equal to or above its previous HFL at any forecasting station.

A computerised monitoring system has been developed under which daily water levels as observed at 0800 hrs. and forecasts issued by field units are transmitted to CWC headquarters in New Delhi. Based on the compilation of all such data received from field divisions, daily water level and flood forecast bulletins in two parts for stage and for inflow forecasting stations respectively. Special Yellow Bulletins are issued whenever the river stage at the forecasting site attains a level within 0.50 m of its previous HFL. Red Bulletins highlighting security of the problem are also issued whenever the water level at the forecasting stations equals or exceeds previous HFL. Bulletins are also updated on CWC Web site: www.cwc.nic.in for wider publicity among user agencies during flood season.

DISASTER PREVENTION AND MITIGATION

The Government of India have adopted mitigation and prevention as essential components of their development strategy. As against the total of 40 million hectares prone to floods, area of about 15 million hectares have been protected by construction of embankments. A number of dams and barrages have been constructed. The State Governments have been assisted to take up mitigation programmes like construction of raised platforms etc. Floods continue to be a menace however mainly because of the huge quantum of silt being carried by the rivers emanating from the Himalayas. This silt has raised the bed level in many rivers to above the level of the countryside. Embankments have also gives rise to problems of drainage with heavy rainfall leading to water logging in areas outside the embankment.

Due to erratic behaviour of monsoons, both low and medium rain fall regions, which constitute about 68% of the total area, are vulnerable to periodical droughts. Our experience has been that almost every third year is a drought year. However, in some of the States, there may be successive drought years enhancing the vulnerability of the population in these areas. Local communities have devised indigenous safety mechanisms and drought oriented farming methods in many parts of the country. From the experience of managing the past droughts particularly the severe drought of 1987, a number of programmes have been launched by the Government to mitigate the impact of drought in the long run. These programmes include Drought Prone Area Programme (DPAP), Desert Development Programme (DDP), National Watershed Development Project for Rainfed Areas (NWDPRA), Watershed Development Programme for Shifting Cultivation (WDPSC), Integrated Water Development Project (IWDP), Integrated Afforestation and Eco-development Project Scheme (IAEPS). A comprehensive programme has been taken up for earthquake mitigation.

Although, the BIS has laid down the standards for construction in the seismic zones, these were not being followed. The building construction in urban and suburban areas is regulated by the Town and Country Planning Acts and Building Regulations. In many cases, the Building regulations do not incorporate the BIS codes. Even where they do, the lack of knowledge regarding seismically safe construction among the architects and engineers as well as lack of awareness regarding their vulnerability among the population led to most of the construction in the urban/sub-urban areas being without reference to BIS standards. In the rural areas, the bulk of the housing is non-engineered construction. The mode of construction in the rural areas has also changed from mud and thatch to brick and concrete construction thereby increasing the vulnerability. The increasing population has led to settlements in vulnerable areas close to the river bed areas which are prone to liquefaction. The Government have moved to address these issues.

A National Core Group for Earthquake Mitigation has been constituted consisting of experts in earthquake engineering and administrators. The Core Group has been assigned with the responsibility of drawing up a strategy and plan of action for mitigating the impact of earthquakes; providing advice and guidance to the States on various aspects of earthquake mitigation; developing/organising the preparation of handbooks/pamphlets/type designs for earthquake resistant construction; working out systems for assisting the States in the seismically vulnerable zones to adopt/integrate appropriate Bureau of Indian Standards codes in their building byelaws; evolving systems for training of municipal engineers as also practicing architects and engineers in the private sector in the salient features of Bureau of Indian Standards codes and the amended byelaws; evolving a system of certification of architects/engineers for testing their knowledge of earthquake resistant construction; evolving systems for training of masons and carry out intensive awareness generation campaigns.

A Committee of experts has been constituted to review the building byelaws. The State Governments have been advised to ensure rigorous enforcement of existing bye laws. A national programme for capacity building for earthquake mitigation has been finalised for imparting training to 10000 engineers in public and private sectors. Since earthquake engineering is not a part of course curriculum in engineering colleges at undergraduate level at present , it is proposed to select 3 to 4 leading engineering colleges in each State and train the faculty members of the civil engineering departments in earthquake engineering at the Indian Institutes of Technology and few other apex level institutes which have the requisite capabilities. These faculty members will take up training of municipal engineers as well as the training of engineers/architects in the private sector in RCC and masonry construction. The first phase of this programme for imparting training to 10000 engineers will be completed within a period of three years. The trained faculty members of the leading engineering colleges will also assist the State Governments in the detailed evaluation of lifeline buildings and their retrofitting, wherever necessary.

It has been decided to include earthquake engineering education in the engineering colleges at undergraduate level. The course curriculum for this purpose has already been finalised by a group of experts taken from IITs and will be introduced in the engineering colleges within an year. A system of special audit of buildings is being put in place with a view to ensuring that the new constructions conform to the latest building byelaws, which have been reviewed and revised recently by Bureau of Indian Standards.

While these mitigation measures will take care of the new constructions, the problem of unsafe existing buildings stock would still remain. It will not be possible to address the entire existing building stock, therefore the life line buildings like hospitals, schools or buildings where people congregate like cinema halls, multi-storied apartments are being focussed on. The States have been advised to have these buildings assessed and where necessary retrofitted. The Ministry of Finance have been requested to advise the financial institutions to give loans for retrofitting on easy terms. Insofar as the private housing stock is concerned emphasis is placed on awareness generation.

An earthquake mitigation project has been finalised for reducing the vulnerability to earthquakes. The programme includes detailed evaluation and retrofitting of lifeline buildings such as hospitals, schools, water and power supply units, telecommunication buildings, airports/airport control towers, railway stations, bus stands and important administrative buildings. The programme also includes training of more than one hundred thousand masons for earthquake resistant constructions. Besides, assistance will be provided under this project to the State Governments to put in place appropriate techno legal regime.

An accelerated urban earthquake vulnerability reduction programme has been taken up in 38 cities in seismic zones III, IV and V with population of half a million and above. Sensitisation workshop for engineers/ architects, government functionaries and voluntary organisations have already been held in 36 of the 38 cities. Disaster mitigation and preparedness plans are under preparation in these cities. Awareness generation campaign has already been undertaken. The orientation courses for engineers and architects have been organised to impart knowledge about seismically safe construction and implementation of BIS norms. This programme will be further extended to 166 earthquake prone districts in seismic zones IV and V.

Rural housing and community assets for vulnerable sections of the population are created at a fairly large scale by the Ministry of Rural Development under the Indira Awas Yojna (IAY) and Sampooran Grameen Rojgar Yojna (SGRY). About 250 thousand small but compact units are constructed every year, besides community assets such as community centres, recreation centres, anganwadi centres etc. Technology support is provided by about two hundred rural housing centres spread over the entire country. The Ministry of Rural Development are now under the process of revising their guidelines for construction of such dwelling units by incorporating appropriate earthquake/cyclone resistant features. Training to the functionaries in the rural housing centres will be organised through the Ministry of Home Affairs. This initiative is expected to go a long way for the construction and popularisation of seismically safe construction at village/block level.

A National Core Group on Cyclone Monitoring and Mitigation has been constituted. Experts from Indian Meteorological Department, National Centre for Medium Range Weather Forecasting, Central Water Commission, National Remote Sensing Agency and Indian Space Research Organisation have been made the Members of the Core Group, besides administrators from the relevant Ministries/Departments and State Governments vulnerable to cyclones. The Group has been assigned with the responsibility of looking warning protocols for cyclones; coordination mechanism between different

Central and State Ministries/Departments/Organisations; mechanism for dissemination of warning to the local people and; cyclone mitigation measures required to be taken for the coastal States. The Group will also suggest short-term and long-term measures on technology upgradation.

A cyclone mitigation project has been formulated. The project inter alia includes components on strengthening of monitoring/warning systems, coastal shelter belt plantation, mangrove plantation, construction of cyclone shelters, storm surge modeling and water envelope studies. The focus will be on regeneration of coastal shelter belt plantation and mangrove plantation where these have degenerated. The location of the cyclone shelters will be decided in such a manner that no person in the vulnerable zone is required to walk more than two kilometers to reach a cyclone shelter. The cyclone shelters will be multi-purpose units to be run as schools or community centres in normal times and will have capacity to house 3000 to 5000 persons with adequate number of toilets, community kitchen and other facilities. Areas will be identified for providing shelter to livestock.

In the engineering designs for construction, special attention will be paid to the attachment of roof to the dwelling units so as to make such units cyclone proof, besides incorporating earthquake resistant features. The project will be taken up shortly and is expected to be completed over a period of five years.

A Disaster Risk Management Programme has been taken up with the assistance from UNDP, USAID and European Union in 169 most hazard prone districts in 17 States including all the 8 North Eastern States. The implementation of the project commenced from October, 2002 and is expected to be concluded by December, 2007. The programme components include awareness generation and public education, preparedness, planning and capacity building, developing appropriate policies, institutional, administrative, legal and techno-legal regime at State, District, Block, village, urban local body and ward levels for vulnerability reduction.

Under this programme Disaster Management Plans have been prepared for about 3500 villages, 250 Gram Panchayat, 60 blocks and 15 districts. Elected representatives of over 8000 Panchayati Raj Institutions have already been trained, besides imparting training to Members of voluntary organisations. Over 20000 Government functionaries have been trained in disaster mitigation and preparedness at different levels. About 600 engineers and 220 architects have been trained under this programme in vulnerability assessment of lifeline buildings.

Training is being imparted to master trainers under the programme. More than 600 master trainers and 1000 teachers have already been trained in different districts in disaster mitigation. Disaster Management Committees consisting of elected representatives, civil society members, Civil Defence volunteers and Government functionaries have been constituted at all levels including village/urban local body/ward levels. Disaster Management Teams have been constituted in villages and are being imparted training in basic functions of first aid, rescue, evacuation and related issues. The thrust of the programme is to build up capabilities of the community since the community is invariably the first responder.

During the last 15 months, it has been experienced that the capacity building of the community has been very helpful even in normal situations when isolated instances of drowning, burns etc. take place. With the creation of awareness generation on disaster mitigation, the community will be able to function as a well-knit unit in case of any emergency. Mock drills are carried out from time to time under the close supervision of Disaster Management Committees. The Disaster Management Committees and Disaster Management Teams have been established by notifications issued by the State Governments which will ensure that the entire system is institutionalised and does not disintegrate after the conclusion of the programme. The key points being stressed under this programme are the need to ensure sustainability of the programme, development of training modules; manuals and codes, up-scaling partnerships in excellence, focused attention to awareness generation campaigns; institutionalisation of disaster management committees and disaster management teams, disaster management plans and mock-drills and establishment of techno-legal regimes.

Human Resource Development at all levels is critical to institutionalisation of disaster mitigation strategy. The National Centre for Disaster Management at the national level has been upgraded and designated as the National Institute of Disaster Management. It is being developed as a Regional Centre of Excellence in Asia. The National Institute of Disaster Management will develop training modules at different levels, undertake training of trainers and organise training programmes for planners, administrators and command functionaries. Besides, the other functions assigned to the National Institute of Disaster Management include development of exhaustive National level information base on disaster management policies, prevention mechanisms, mitigation measures; formulation of disaster management code and providing consultancy to various States in strengthening their disaster management systems and capacities as well as preparation of disaster management plans and strategies for hazard mitigation and disaster response.

Disaster Management faculties have already been created in 29 State level training institutes located in 28

States. These faculties are being directly supported by the Ministry of Home Affairs. The State Training Institutions take up several focused training programmes for different target groups within the State. The Disaster Management faculties in these Institutes are being further strengthened so as to enable them to develop as Institutes of Excellence for a specific disaster. This system has already been institutionalised and is being further strengthened so as to make it a focal point in each State for development of human resources in disaster mitigation and preparedness. Assistance to the State level training institutes will be provided by the National Institute of Disaster Management in the development of training/capsules training modules for different functionaries at different levels.

Bibliography

Abramovitz, Janet, "Unnatural disasters", *Worldwatch Paper*, 2001.

Adams, Robin and Spence, Robin, *Earthquake*, Ingleton, J. (Ed.), 1999.

Benn, D. and Hall, K., *Globalization, A Calculus of Inequality*, Published by Ian Randle Publishers, Jamaica, 2000.

Benson, C., "Disaster Management", *Pro-poor Infrastructure Provision*, Keysheet 2. Draft, 2002.

Blaikie, P., Cannon,T., Davis, I. and Wisner, B., *At Risk: Natural Hazards, People's Vulnerability, and Disasters*, Routledge, London and New York, 1996.

Burton, I., Kates, R., White, G.F., *The Environment as Hazard*, The Guildford Press, New York. 2nd Edition. 1993.

Christoplos, Ian; Mitchell, John and Liljelund, Anna, "Re-framing Risk: The Changing Context of Disaster Mitigation and Preparedness", In *Disasters*, Volume 25, No.3, September 2001.

Cordery, I and Pilgrim, D.H., "The State of the Art of Flood Prediction", *In Floods*, Volume 2, 185-197. Edited by Parker, D. Routledge, London. 2000.

Cuny, Fred, *Disasters and Development*, Oxford University, 1983.

Hewitt, K., *Regions at Risk*, Longman, London, 1996.

Ingleton, J., *Natural Disaster Management*, Tudor Rose, Leicester, 1999.

Maskrey, A., *Reducing Global Disasters*, 1999.

McGregor, A.M. and McGregor, I.K.L., "Disasters and Agriculture in the Pacific Islands", *United Nations Disaster Management*

Programme - South Pacific Office (UNDMP-SPO), South Pacific Disaster Reduction Programme (RAS/92/360), 1999.

Mileti, D.S., *Disasters by Design: A Reassessment of Natural Hazards in the United States*, Joseph Henry Press, Washington, DC, 1999.

Platt, R.H., *Disasters and Democracy*, Island Press,Washington DC, 1999.

Rosenthal, U., Boin, Arjen, Comfort, R. and L., *Managing Crisis*, Published by Charles Thomas, Springfield. USA, 2001.

Smith, Keith, *Environmental Hazards*, Second Edition. Routledge, London and New York, 1996.

Tierney, Kathleen, "Trends in Research and Disaster Management in the United States", In *Natural Hazards Observer*, Volume 26, Number 1, September 2001.

Trujillo, M., Ordonez, A., Hernandez, C., *Risk Mapping and Local Capacities: Lessons from Mexico and Central America Oxfam*, Oxford. 2000.

Twigg, John and Bhatt, Mihir R., *Understanding Vulnerability: South Asian Perspectives*, Intermediate Technology Publications and Duryog Nivaren, London and Columbo, 1998.

Index

37. Indian Polity **(Revised Edition)** 295/-
38. New Comparative Government **(Revised Edition)** 295/-

Advanced Study in the History of Modern India

39. (Volume-1: 1707–1813) 225/-
40. (Volume-2: 1813–1920) 325/-
41. (Volume-3: 1920–1947) 175/-
42. Handbook of Nutrition & Dietetics 250/-
43. Development of Education in India 195/-
44. A Textbook of Environment Studies 195/-
45. Teaching of History 175/-
46. Administrative Thinkers 195/-
47. Research Methodology 175/-
48. Curriculum Development 195/-
49. Teaching of Science 175/-
50. Teaching of Mathematics 175/-
51. Principles of Educational & Vocational Guidance 195/-
52. Child Psychology 175/-
53. Abnormal Psychology 175/-
54. Indian Education in Emerging Society 195/-
55. Human Resource Management 175/-
56. Higher Education and Global challenges 175/-
57. Teaching of Geography 175/-
58. Teaching of Social Studies 175/-
59. Teaching of English 175/-
60. PrincipleofOffceManagement(RevisedEdition) 250/-
61. Education for All The Indian Saga 175/-
62. Value Education in Global Perspective 195/-
63. Teacher Training 175/-
64. Public Administration 175/-
65. Public Relations & Integrated Communications 195/-
66. Educational Psychology 175/-
67. Introduction to Educational Technology 175/-
68. Textbook of Food and Nutrition 175/-

Unit No. 220, 2nd Floor, 4735/22,
Prakash Deep Building, Ansari Road, Darya Ganj,
New Delhi - 110002, Ph.: 32903912, 23280047, 09811594448
E-mail: lotus_press@sify.com, www.lotuspress.co.in